HOW TO SOAR
WITH THE EAGLES

HOW TO SOAR
WITH THE EAGLES

Peter Legge
with
Duncan Holmes

EAGLET PUBLISHING

Eaglet Publishing
401, 4180 Lougheed Highway
Burnaby, British Columbia, V5C 6A7 Canada

Canadian Cataloguing in Publication Data

Legge, Peter, 1942-
    How to soar with the eagles

    1. Success.   2. Self-actualization (Psychology).
I. Holmes, Duncan.   II. Title.
BF637.S8L43 1991   158'.1   C91-091498-2

Includes index
ISBN 0-9695447-0-7

First Printing   August 1991
Second Printing   September 1992
Third Printing   September 1993
Fourth Printing   December 1994

Jacket design by Catherine Mullaly
Typeset by Sheila Lloyd
Edited by Sheila Jones of International Wordsmiths Ltd.
Printed and bound in Canada by Friesen Printers

*Dedicated to
my beloved
wife Kay and the
three treasures of my life
my magnificent daughters
Samantha, Rebecca and Amanda*

CONTENTS

Introduction   *11*

1.   Why God, Why?   *15*

2.   The Reading Edge   *19*

3.   "Mr. Legge! Nice to See You!"   *23*

4.   Tomorrow, Drive *Forward!*   *25*

5.   Open Your Eyes, People!   *29*

6.   The Night Nobody Laughed   *33*

7.   Making Something out of Nothing   *37*

8.   50 Quotations for Life   *41*

9.   Coming Home First Class   *49*

10.   The Man at the Palace   *51*

11.   Give a Little, Get a Lot   *55*

12.   Frank Rethinks Life   *57*

13.   Life is for the Future   *61*

14.   What are *You* Hiding?   *65*

15.   Taking on Goliath   *69*

16.   Eppich Proportion   *73*

17.   Don't Judge a Cockney   *77*

18.   Service with a Shine   *81*

19.   What Are You Building?   *85*

20.   How's Your Memory?   *87*

21.   10 Ways to Help You Soar   *91*

22.   Bamboo Wisdom   *95*

23.   Teeing up for Life   97
24.   31,000 Days!   101
25.   Learning Louie Lore   103
26.   Top Line!   107
27.   It's a Long Way to London   109
28.   Take a Christmas Break   113
29.   *It's Showtime!*   119
30.   Back to Tavistock Hall   123
31.   "Good Morning, God!"   129
32.   Kick the Tires of Your Day   133
33.   Trust: A Paris Touch   139
34.   Murray Plays His Strongest Suit   143
35.   Plain Gold Band   147
36.   The Extra Mile   151
37.   Going to the Mountaintop   153
38.   Do You Have All Your Marbles?   157
39.   "As a Man Thinketh"   161
40.   Let's Get Physical!   163
41.   Making the Most of *OG*ortunity   167
42.   Opportunityisnowhere!   171
43.   Be Thankful for Your Troubles   173
44.   Minuet at Cecil Green   175
45.   The Big Picture from Gastown   181
46.   Good Heavens, It's Friday!   189
47.   "No Man is an Island"   195

ACKNOWLEDGEMENTS

As you will quickly discover in this book, my life has been influenced by many people whose words, thoughts and actions have made me listen, think, and sometimes move in new directions. Others, a special few, have given me powerful, life-long encouragement and inspiration. With pride, I include among this latter group my parents, Bernie and Win Legge, who from my earliest remembered years were not just parents, but friends, who gave me every chance to run with my life, to be there to support my adventures and enterprise, to give me encouragement, to offer consolation when it was needed, to give freely and often of their wisdom and love. I thank them from my heart for all of that.

To my friend Duncan Holmes, who helped to work the words of this book, I offer similar thanks. In many ways, Duncan and I think the same way, but it takes his kind of magic touch to bring the ideas together. We had some delightful meetings and a number of very memorable lunches.

I thank Karen Foss and Neil Soper, Executive Vice Presidents of Canada Wide Magazines for their continuing support and encouragement in business and in this book. I thank Corinne Smith, Trish Campbell, Rick Butler, Jennifer Holmes and Joyce Robinson, who each made important individual contributions.

Lastly and collectively I acknowledge all of those people whose stories we have included. Perhaps more than anyone, they are the ones who inspired us to begin.

Peter Legge
Vancouver, B.C.

Introduction

AT THE HEAD OF HOWE SOUND just north of Vancouver, British Columbia, the Squamish River flows into the sea.

Into the Squamish, after cutting its tortuous way through the canyons of the coast range, flows the Cheakamus.

And into the Cheakamus, along with hundreds of other bubbling streams fed by the mists, rain and snow that cloak and pummel this craggy part of Canada flows the Tenderfoot.

Among world rivers, the Tenderfoot is insignificant. It snakes along at the bottom of the mountains, churns through the narrows, surges across the occasional flatlands. It's pretty, but on a fast ride to the nearby Whistler snow country, you'd never know it was there.

But the salmon do. The chum, coho and chinook that live in the ocean wilderness of the North Pacific, that are mysteriously drawn back to the streams of their birth, that escape the technology of the fishing industry along the way, they know the Tenderfoot. The salmon come back to its quiet gravels to spawn and to die.

And around Christmas every year, hundreds of bald eagles fly in to feast on the dead and dying salmon. You can go in and see them. Tenderfoot Creek near the village of Brackendale, opens up a bit into a lake — more like a large pond — right near a federal government salmon hatchery. For those who yearn to see these proud birds, they are there, sitting on the branches of the cedar, fir and hemlock — as bald as all get out and stuffed with salmon.

While it's a powerful experience to see that many eagles all at once, it's a bit of a letdown that they're all so accessible — they are, after all wild creatures. You can get quite close, take pictures, watch them watching you. It's a giant aviary without the confining cover.

Early in the year, round about the time the Christmas bills start coming in, the feast is done and the eagles and the people leave, allowing the Tenderfoot to end the winter and to nurse a new salmon generation of eggs to life.

Whatever we imagine wildlife to be, I think we imagine it best when it flies high and swims or runs free. Eagles are our inspiration when they kick off from the high crags, spread their immense wings, catch the thermals and open their eyes to the widest horizons. Salmon are our inspiration when they are silver and strong, coursing great arcs of ocean, mysterious new channels of marine discovery.

We are fascinated as the cycles of these creatures

meet in a place like Tenderfoot Creek — but it is fascination tinged with a certain sadness, a melange of death and easy pickings.

The eagles we love are those that stretch and soar. The salmon we remember are creatures not of decay, but of sparkling, muscled silver. I have no idea how the rest of the animal kingdom thinks, but I suspect that the eagles and the salmon enjoy life a lot more than the times they spend together at Tenderfoot Creek.

This is not a book about eagles, but a lot of it is about what I believe the eagles do for each of us. Get us away from the easy pools and take us to the mountaintops. Way up there in their craggy aeries, we can, through an eagle's eye, look on life with a new perspective. Be challenged by what lies beyond the next mountain, across the next valley.

This is a book of stories about people and events that have given me inspiration, each a new lesson in the challenge that is life.

I've always found that just about everyone has a better idea than I do and it's always worth listening to discover what those ideas are all about. Similarly, every person who is succeeding has some kind of a secret that he or she feels has contributed to that success. There are icons and words and mentors — and I watch and constantly listen for them, and in my presentations and in this book, I share the best of them.

Some are attributed. Others are scraps of anonymous wisdom or the work of others that has come to me unattributed. I would like nothing more than to give credit where it is so obviously due. If you are able to help in any of these situations, I will be delighted to rectify the authorship in subsequent editions.

I have heard many successful, self-motivated people say that the fun is not in the having, but in the getting. Flying is a great reward for a fledgling eagle, but so too is the struggle.

I DO hope you enjoy this book, that somewhere in its pages there may be a thought, a breeze that will be the wind beneath YOUR wings.

The eagles of Tenderfoot Creek are, after all, only pausing. Their life flight will go on — across the valleys, beyond the mountains, on to the most distant and challenging horizons.

We can watch. Or we too can fly.

Peter Legge
Vancouver, B.C. Canada, July, 1991

CHAPTER 1

Why God, Why?

ON JANUARY 17, 1991, when I was in the middle of writing this book, the United Nations Coalition Forces, with the backing of all necessary authority, started a military action to remove the occupying army of Iraq from Kuwait.

It was war.

The decade changed, the century changed, and we were changed. Despite our distance from the Middle East theatre, we could not have been emotionally closer if we had tried. Through television, the war grabbed us and ate us up.

We pulled out maps of a region that in previous days could have been made for the surface of Mars. We related Baghdad to Tel Aviv and Riyadh to the rest of sprawling Saudi Arabia. We talked about war with our families, our fellow workers. We had knowledge of its consequences, its horrific real and imagined power. It spread blackness over all of our lives.

Some of us had known war of this kind before and we believed that perhaps we had learned its lessons. If you keep talking, we always said, if you maintain pressure, if your cause is just, then the fatal day might be avoided.

As tanks rolled into Kuwait and the bombs fell on Baghdad, others asked how it could have happened. Still others sought answers from God.

For some time, among my personal papers, I have had a copy of an anonymous poem that often seems to fit the struggle of humanity. When the war started, I pulled it out and read it again.

Its question, like that of many of us at a time like this, is "Why?" I pass the question on.

I walked today through the slums of life,
Down the dark streets of wretchedness, and of pain.
I trod today where few have trod
and as I walked I challenged God.

I saw the sots in the bar rooms.
I saw the prostitutes in the dance halls.
I saw the thieves as they picked pockets.
I saw men and women devoid of life,
     living in a world of sin,
and above the din I whispered, "Why God, Why?"

I walked today down the lanes of hate,
Hearing the jeers of bitter men,
Hearing the names as they cursed and spat
"Dago, Nigger, Kike, Jap."
I saw the defected men they stoned.
I felt the anguish of their cries.
I saw them as they slapped the lonely,
as they turned their backs on human needs.
Snarling, growling were the fiends of hell.
These, God called his sons!
Gasping for air, I cried "Why God, Why?"

I walked today through wars of grim dregs . . .
over graveless men.
I saw the dead, the crucified, the headless,
the limbless, the pleading, the crying.
I saw the pain, the waste.
I smelled the odor of rotted flesh.

I saw the children gathered round
. . . watching, naked, hungry, weeping, diseased,
*   dirty . . .*
The baby trying to nurse from a dead mother.
The ruins . . . the agony . . . the despair!
Disaster . . . disaster . . . all around!

Blinded with tears, I fled down these streets.
I stumbled, then stopped.
I shouted "Why God, Why?"
Why do you let man sin, hate and suffer?
Unmerciful Father! God, are you blind?
Are you wicked and cruel?

God, can you watch and do nothing?
Why must this be?

The world grew silent.
I awaited reply.
The silence was heavy.
I started to tremble.
I waited long . . . half rebuking, half fearing,
Then I heard from close behind me
"Why . . . Man . . . Why?"

CHAPTER 2

The Reading Edge

Several years ago in a superb speech he made to a convention in Chicago, I learned a valuable lesson from a man called Joel Weldon, a powerful motivational speaker from Arizona.

"If the average book has 250 pages and you read 12 pages a day," said Joel, "you will read 17 1/2 books a year."

Simple, profound, good advice.

Then I heard Brian Tracey, one of North America's foremost educators and trainers, and he took it a bit further.

Read for an hour a day, he said, and that adds up to a book a week or 50 books a year. In five to 10 years you will have read 500 to 1,000 books — compared with the North American average of one book per person per year.

Does reading give you an edge? Of course it does.

Within three years you could be an expert on your chosen subject matter in your community, in five years an expert in your country and in 10 years, an expert internationally.

In 1936, Dale Carnegie first published How to Win Friends and Influence People. It has become an international best seller, a classic in its field.

Amazing as it seems, Carnegie didn't even want to publish his book, but despite the passage of more than 50 years of world change, How to Win Friends has maintained a leadership position virtually unmatched in the publishing industry. Its cumulative sales total 15 million world wide.

How to Win Friends is a book of simple language, easy to understand thoughts, dozens of quotations from others. The first time round it was not well received. Reviewers, intellectuals and journalists saw it as a manifestation of the decline of public taste.

But after the sale of 500,000 copies, Carnegie was invited to speak to the Dutch Treat Club in New York, a club of editors, publishers, advertising people and others who were interested in the book's success, but cynical about its literary merit. Carnegie knew they were ready to eat him alive.

He opened with this statement.

"I know there's considerable criticism of my book. People say I'm not profound and there's nothing in it new to psychology and human relations.

"This is true. Gentlemen, I have never claimed to have a new idea. Of course I deal with the obvious. I present, reiterate and glorify the obvious because the obvious is what people need to be told. The greatest need of people is to know how to deal with other people. This should come naturally to them but it doesn't.

"I am told that you are a hostile audience. But I plead not guilty. The ideas I stand for are not mine. I borrowed them from Socrates, I swiped them from Chesterfield, I stole them from Jesus and I put them in a book. If you don't like THEIR rules, whose would you use? I would be glad to listen."

According to William Longgood, Carnegie's official biographer, he received a thunderous ovation.

To some degree this book, and much of the content of many of my speaking engagements, is an accumulation of proven and reliable ideas learned from other people, life tested in my own business and personal experience.

The sources become vague, but I know that I draw on a list that includes Dale Carnegie, Zig Ziglar, Brian Tracey, Chuck Swindoll, Chuck Ferguson, Joel Weldon, Mark MacCormick, Og Mandino, Earl Nightingale, Napleon Hill, W. Clement Stone, Dr. Norman Vincent Peale and many, many more.

I salute and say thanks to these fine educators, motivational leaders, speakers and trainers of the human spirit. They have influenced me and taught me much. As Dale Carnegie said, the ideas may not be new, but each eagerly awaited presentation is refreshment for the soul.

Mine is a life being lived to the full and this book shares thoughts from that joyous experience. If within its pages you discover a dividend of teaching, I shall be richly blessed.

CHAPTER 3

"Mr. Legge! Nice to See You!"

A QUICKIE ABOUT FOUR IMPORTANT WORDS that will help you achieve and maintain success.

The first two are your client's first and last names.

You may be saying: "Hey, I've got 600 clients, who do you think I am?"

If you have 600 clients or 10,000 customers, terrific. All I'm suggesting is that when you're meeting a client or a customer, make sure you remember that client's name and use it often during your meeting.

People love being called by name.

"Good evening, Mr. Legge, your table is ready."

"Mr. Legge! Nice to see you again."

Carry a 'cheat sheet' if you must, but get involved with names.

(I play a little name game with my wife for the times I forget names of people I should know. If she notices I'm not using the name of a client or I have not introduced her, she moves right in and introduces herself, which quickly elicits the name of the client. Which in turn gets the line from me: "Oh Bill, I didn't realize that you and Kay hadn't met." Phew!)

The other two words, not surprisingly, are please and thankyou. I am amazed how many business men and women, particularly those who are both middle aged and middle management and above, seem to have forgotten these two simple, powerful words.

Whether you are talking to your receptionist, your secretary, the maitre d', your boss, your wife, or your children, please and thankyou are a vital part of the language of business and common courtesy.

Without them, there's a vacuum. With them, there is an immediate understanding that the other person has an appreciation for whatever it is you have done.

Regardless of the city, the country, the predicament, bring these four great words into your language. And be prepared for the smiles.

CHAPTER 4

Tomorrow, Drive *Forward!*

I KNOW PEOPLE WHO ARE SO UNEXCITED about life that the first thing they do when they get up in the morning is start making plans about going to bed that night.

Can you believe it!

Where's the enthusiasm? Where's the commitment to the life that God gave them?

It CAN be tough to start a new day, but if we never do anything about changing the way that our potentially great days can unfold, we can die in the process.

Try this on for size.

Tomorrow, pick a person in your life who you'll be dealing with for most of the day and deal with him or her as though he or she will die at midnight.

Don't panic, it's not for real!

But think about what you're doing. You're going to talk and interact with that person in a substantially different way.

Perhaps for the first time, you'll really be paying attention to who that person really is. You'll look him or her right in the eye. You'll ask a lot of caring questions about what makes them tick, what their dreams and goals are, what excites them in life.

They will respond to you in a totally different way because, perhaps for the first time, they will say: "Hey, this person really cares about me."

When we react in life nothing much happens. When we respond in life, amazing things happen. People respond to you when they know that you really care. And people don't care how much you know until they know how much you care. Think about that.

And starting tomorrow — after 21 days it will become a habit! — give thanks and be grateful for five things in your life.

As you pull on your socks or take a shower or wait for your toast, say them out loud. It will clear your head, focus your attitude, get you going. Forget about the things you don't have. Someday, they too will be on your list.

And just for a change, back your car into the garage tonight. Tomorrow morning, you'll drive into your new world front first and feel better because of it! Who needs to back into a day!

A quick story to keep the ball of enthusiasm rolling.

A fifty-year-old man went to his doctor for a check-up. (Yep, it's another checkup joke!) And the doctor, filling in some of the details, asked: "At what age did your father die?"

"My father's not dead," said the patient, "He's 75

years old."

"O.K., when did your grandfather die?"

"He's not dead either, he's 97 years old."

Slightly taken aback, the doctor asked: "So when did your great-grandfather die?"

"My great-grandfather," said the patient, "is 115 years old and two weeks from today he's getting married!"

"Good heavens," said the doctor, "why would a 115-year-old man want to get married?"

"Want?" asked the patient. "Who said anything about him wanting to get married?"

I love that story.

Remember five things you're thankful for. Nice loud voice. Drive forward from the garage. And make it a great day!

CHAPTER 5

Open Your Eyes, People!

ALBERT EINSTEIN was once asked for his definition of the purpose of life.

Surprisingly, or perhaps not, Einstein said: "The purpose of life is to serve mankind."

If I've achieved any form of success in my career, it is due in part to coming to grips with Einstein's statement.

In business, it's natural to 'serve' our customers, providing them with exactly what they need, understanding the Nineties terminology of 'value added' with each sale.

But I have also discovered that giving back to the community as much or more than you take out is more in keeping with Einstein's statement.

In the last 15 years, I've discovered my business has grown in direct proportion to the amount of community and charity work I've undertaken.

Zig Ziglar, one of North America's foremost

motivational speakers and seminar leaders, said: "You can get everything you want in life if you just help enough people get what THEY want in life."

This is not to say that you should become involved with 101 charities and your business will automatically prosper. But look for a couple of organizations that would benefit from your expertise, then commit a significant amount of time — to serve, not to benefit.

The benefits will astound you; the people you meet will have a profound affect on your life.

Variety Club International is such an organization. Variety dedicates itself in 15 countries to aiding less abled children. It helps them to fight for independence, to understand the importance of realizing their potential, to establish a meaningful life, to integrate, where possible, with society and be accepted for their differences.

In Variety, many individuals have tugged at my heartstrings and made an impact on my life.

But let me tell you about one helping person who is very special. If you watch Variety Club Telethons just about anywhere in North America — from New York to Toronto to Des Moines to Vancouver — you will have seen my dear friend Lee Bussard.

Lee has cerebral palsy. He says if you can say it, you don't have it. He is married to Pat, they have two beautiful children and he is one of North America's most sought after motivational speakers who champions the cause for the physically challenged.

Lee played ice hockey for eight years and wore snowmobile boots as a goalie. He says he shook so much in the net that nobody knew where to shoot the puck.

Lee has triumphed over his obvious handicap. But the more time you spend with him, the less you notice that he is any different than you are.

Almost without exception when Lee appears on a Variety Club telethon, the phone pledges take an immediate jump following his reading of the poem he made famous. With his kind permission, I share it with you.

A Handicapped Person Wrote This

What do you see people, what do you see?
What are you thinking when you are looking
        at me . . .
A handicapped person, not very wise
Uncertain of habit, with far away eyes,
Who dribbles food and makes no reply
When you say in a loud voice . . ."I do
        wish you'd try."
Who seems not to notice the things that you do,
And forever is losing a stocking or shoe.
Who unresisting or not, lets you do as you will,
With bathing and feeding, the long day to fill.
Is that what you're thinking, is that what you see?
Then open your eyes, people, you're not looking at
        me.
I'll tell you who I am as I sit here so still . . .
As I rise at your bidding, as I eat at your will.
I'm a small child of ten with a father and mother,
Brothers and sisters, who love one another.
A person of sixteen with wings on their feet,
Dreaming that soon now a lover they'll meet.

Married soon at twenty . . . my heart gives a leap,
Remembering the vows that I promised to keep.

At twenty-five, now I have young of my own,
Who need me to build a secure happy home.
A person of thirty, my young now grow fast . . .
Bound to each other with ties that should last.
At forty, my young sons have grown and are gone,
But my mate's beside me to see I don't mourn.
At fifty, once more babies play round my knee,
Again we know children, my loved one and me.
Dark days are upon me, my mate is dead,
I look at the future, I shudder with dread.
For my young are all rearing young of their own,
And I think of the years and the love that I've
        known.
I'm an old person now, and nature is cruel —
"Tis people jest to make old age look like a fool."
The body is crumpled, grace and vigor depart,
There is now a stone where I once had a heart.
But inside this old carcass a person still dwells,
And now and again my battered heart swells.
I remember the joys, I remember the pain,
And I'm loving and living life over again.
I think of the years all too few — gone too fast,
So open your eyes people, open and see, not a
        handicapped person
Look closer — see me.

Get involved with those who need your help and
your love. You MAY touch THEIR lives. They will
CERTAINLY touch YOURS.

CHAPTER 6

The Night Nobody Laughed

IN THE COURSE OF WRITING THIS BOOK, I had the thought that I was creating a very distinct impression that nothing ever goes wrong in the life of Legge.

One DOES tend to focus on the positive in a book like this. Everything comes out completely upbeat, a reflection of endless success, impeccable timing, complete control — never a hint that anything ever goes wrong, or that from time to time there may even be the occasional embarrassing moment.

Let me tell you a story that will help balance the scales.

At one stage in my life, I sought a career in the United Kingdom as a comedian. I had had some success making people laugh and figured that with a bit of British luck, I'd go straight to the top.

But in show business, there are always dues to pay. Anyone who has ever made it will tell you stories of dingy dressing rooms, ruthless theatre operators and, worst of all, audiences that eat you alive.

So here I was down in the depths of darkest Wales, doing a circuit of 20 working men's clubs for six pounds a night, trying to get blokes who had been down the mine all day to enjoy a few laughs with a beer. I knew nothing about Wales, couldn't pronounce the names of half the towns I was visiting and knew even less of the local lore and legends.

But that didn't seem too important. Humor has universal appeal and on one rainy night in a small Welsh village, right after the singer and the magician, on came Peter.

I went right into my jokes about kids. Hard driving stories about how rotten they can be, how ungrateful and unnecessary they really are. Real funny stuff that had cracked 'em up in London.

Not a laugh. Not even a murmur of a laugh. And 12 minutes later, I gave up, walked off the stage, right into the arms of the furious club owner.

"On your way, mate," he said without further explanation. Clenched mouth, fierce eyes. "Outta town!"

Hurt, puzzled and upset at the lack of response to what I knew was a proven routine, I slunk back to the hotel.

"Aberfan," I said, reading the signs on the stores in the high street. "Aberfan."

And it all clicked and I knew what had gone wrong.

A month before, from high on a hill above the town's small primary school, a tip, the monstrous leftover pile from the diggings in a coalmine, had slipped and raced down the hillside. It slid like a great grey blanket over the school and took the lives of 170 people, most of them children, in the worst disaster of its kind in history.

Many of the working men in the club that night were fathers of those children — still filled with memories of the faces and lives of those young Welsh citizens who had died beneath the Aberfan tip. I felt absolutely awful.

It IS important to know where you are and to have some knowledge about what's going on. If you don't, as I found out that night, you get exactly what you deserve.

I've never forgotten that Aberfan audience. In a special way, I will share their grief for the rest of my life.

CHAPTER 7

Making Something out of Nothing

I'VE ALWAYS BELIEVED that we have the potential to achieve our brilliant best when we are in the midst of adversity. When we're down in the dumps, when we seem to have hit a cycle of failure, we also have the potential to kick into some long lost resources to make something happen.

Similarly, if we go through life with our eyes wide open, there are many times when we can seize opportunity — make something out of seemingly nothing.

Six months before EXPO 86 opened in Vancouver and set the town on its ear, I had the good fortune to be sitting on a beach in Hawaii having a holiday. As often happens on holidays, I was resting my body, but my brain continued to spin ideas. It's an insistent computer that disregards warm trade winds and cool Mai Tais to keep on churning. And I'm glad it does.

The thought was mostly a passive one, but I know

that what I was looking for was an opportunity to link some kind of business venture with what I believed would be a highly successful world exposition. Like the builder of the Field of Dreams, I felt that if I had the right product, the people would come.

It's funny how the subconscious works, but in the brilliance of a Waikiki afternoon in that November vacation, the IDEA came. And the idea presented the opportunity.

Knowing that EXPO 86's special visitors would include Prince Charles and Princess Diana, my plan would be to publish a souvenir book on their visit to British Columbia. The world loved them, and the world, with luck and good management, would love my book.

Two weeks later, having struck a deal with a photographer to share in the speculation, and the book's potential success, I was on a plane to London. There at the British Information Office, I dived into the public domain photographs on the life and times of the royal couple and, at no charge, swept up the best of the stock material that would allow the project to begin.

In any venture of this kind, it's comforting and fiscally prudent to have as much money as possible up front to pay the bills. It's good business and it's common sense. There's nothing worse than having to gamble on unknown sales, to be left at the end of the day with unsaleable books and unpayable bills.

With all that in mind, I decided that even if I didn't yet have a book, I could still pre-SELL a book and in January and February of EXPO year, with two months to go before the fair was due to open, I started running ads.

For just $9.95, the ads said, you can own a spectacular souvenir limited edition hardcover book that will celebrate the visit to EXPO 86 of Their Royal Highnesses Prince Charles and Princess Diana. We would accept credit cards, cheques and cash.

By the end of February, we had 2,000 orders and almost $20,000 in the bank. Encouraging? It was beyond belief! When weeks later the total hit $30,000, I knew we had a potential winner.

As the ad campaign continued to pile up orders and with them the funds to finance the program, the production work went on in the background. Credentials were arranged for writers and photographers; design people were beginning to assemble the known and unknown materials; printers were being organized for what I hoped would be the fastest turnaround in the history of lithography.

Distribution was being arranged throughout the EXPO 86 grounds. The book — and we weren't even close at that stage to having a sample — would be available in the British Pavilion, in all of the other Commonwealth pavilions, in all of the fair's souvenir outlets.

When the Royals arrived, our team had credentials to follow them like hawks, to shoot every move, even as the words were beginning to come together that would give the book its special substance, its elements of salability, of memorability.

With superhuman effort from a lot of people — from the creative team to the production crew, to the drivers who headed back through the night from printing facilities in Winnipeg — we were 'on the street' two weeks after the tour of Prince Charles and Princess Diana had ended.

It WAS a smash hit. Sales totalled in excess of $500,000 and I'm happy to report that the only copies still unsold are the 10 that are kept under lock and key in my office.

We sent special copies by courier to Buckingham Palace, to President Reagan, to Prime Ministers Mulroney of Canada, Hawke of Australia and Thatcher of Great Britain. Each acknowledged the gift, but it was Mrs. Thatcher who wrote us a personal letter, something I shall always remember with deepest gratitude.

Another satisfying aspect to all of this was the program initiated to support Pearson College of the Pacific on Vancouver Island — part of the United World Colleges network, of which none other than Prince Charles himself is chairman.

Vancouver businessman Ray Addington, a good friend who along the way earned himself an Order of the British Empire for his good works, was in charge of fund raising for Pearson College. Following up on his initiative, the book become a focal point for sales and fund raising, especially when Prince Charles was gracious enough to include a letter that became part of the book. The college benefitted to the tune of $70,000!

You CAN lift yourself out of the dumps. It may be as simple as walking around the block and opening your eyes to a world that always offers something new, of setting the simplest goal to make things better than they were.

And you CAN seize opportunities. They are not always big ones and sometimes you have to seek them out. But finding them, running with them to the end of the road — the rewards can be powerfully exciting.

40

CHAPTER 8

50 Quotations for Life

IT'S SAFE TO SAY that all wise thoughts have already been thought more or less the same way many thousands of times.

To make someone else's wise thought part of OUR thinking, we must read it, re-read it and absorb its meaning. In time it becomes part of our personal experience.

These thoughts have come into my life. You may wish to make them part of yours.

This is the day which the Lord hath made; we will rejoice and be glad in it.

Psalm 118:24

Some men see things as they are and ask "Why?" I see them as they have never been and ask, "Why not?"

George Bernard Shaw

Nothing great was ever achieved without enthusiasm.

Ralph Waldo Emerson

A man can succeed at almost anything for which he has unlimited enthusiasm.

Charles M. Schwab

Never, never, never, never give up.

Sir Winston Churchill

I am not interested in the past. I am interested in the future, for that is where I expect to spend the rest of my life.

Charles F. Kettering

What lies behind you what lies ahead of you pales in comparison with what lies within you.

Ralph Waldo Emerson

Accept neither success nor failure. Neither need be permanent.

Bernard Legge

I have come that you might live life in all its fullness.

John 10:10

Act as if it were impossible to fail.

Dorothea Brande

The greatest discovery of my generation is that a human being can alter his life by altering his attitude of mind.

William James

Men are born to succeed, not to fail.

Henry David Thoreau

You can have everything in life you want if you help enough other people get what they want.

Zig Ziglar

It's a funny thing about life; if you refuse to accept anything but the best, you very often get it.

W. Somerset Maugham

The Serenity Prayer: God grant me the serenity to accept the things I cannot change, courage to change the things I can and wisdom to know the difference.

Reinhold Niebuhr

People who think they can and people who think they can't are probably right.

Henry Ford

We are or become those things which we repeatedly do. Therefore, excellence can become not just an event but a habit.

Albert Einstein

For as he thinketh in his heart, so he is.

Proverbs 23:7

Our life is what our thoughts make it.

Marcus Aurelius Antoninus

The thought is the ancestor of the deed.

Thomas Carlyle

Where there is no vision, people perish.

Proverbs 29:18

Too many people have their competition manage their affairs . . . manage your own.

It's not good enough to do our best. Sometimes we have to do what is required.

Sir Winston Churchill

Press on.
Nothing in the world can take the place of persistence.
Talent will not.
Unrewarded genius is almost a proverb.
Education will not.
The world is full of educated derelicts.
Persistence and determination alone are important.

Calvin Coolidge

If you don't know where you're going, you'll probably end up someplace else.

Yogi Berra

Every man is enthusiastic at times.
One man has enthusiasm for 30 minutes.
Another has it for 30 days.
But it's the man that has it for 30 years
who make a success in life.

The Catholic Layman

44

Don't wait for your ship to come in. Swim out to it.

Anonymous

You cannot perform in a manner inconsistent with the way you see yourself.

To be enthusiastic, act enthusiastic!

You'll go out on a limb sometimes because that's where the fruit is!

Will Rogers

If one advances confidently in the direction of his dreams, and endeavors to live the life he has imagined, he will meet with a success unexpected in common hours.

Henry David Thoreau

Success is the progressive realization of a worthy idea or goal.

Earl Nightingale

The only way to fail at prospecting is to avoid it.

The Winner never Quits — And the Quitter never Wins!

William E. Holler

As I grow older, I pay less attention to what men say — I simply watch what they do.

Andrew Carnegie

The past is important, but it is not nearly as important to your present as is the way you see your future.

Dr. Tony Campolo

You are what you are and where you are because of what's gone into your mind.

You can change what you are and where you are by changing what goes into your mind.

Zig Ziglar

Change your thoughts and you change your world.

Norman Vincent Peale

Our thoughts are traitors and make us lose the good we oft might win by fearing to attempt.

William Shakespeare

If a man asks you to go a mile with him, go two miles.

Jesus Christ

Attitudes are more important than facts.

Karl Menninger M.D.

Would the child you once were be proud of the person you have become?

In the long run, men hit only what they aim at.

Henry David Thoreau

It's amazing how much people can get done if they do not worry about who gets the credit.

Sandra Swinney
(This quote is said to have been framed and sat on
the desk of former U.S. President Ronald Reagan).

People are failures, not because they are stupid, but because they are not sufficiently impassioned.

Bert Struthers

The most important weapon on earth is the human soul on fire.

Ferdinand Foch

It's not what happens to you, it's what you make of it.

As we see people, we treat them;
And as we treat them, often they become.

As you might imagine yourself to be, so in time you will become.

He who has a *Why* to live for can bear almost any *How.*

Nietzche

CHAPTER 9

Coming Home First Class

BUSINESS LEADERS are always looking for innovative ways to stimulate their employees — the people who collectively do much to make things happen.

In today's shrinking world, the airlines are used a lot by business. Getting from A to B quickly and comfortably is most important. The airlines know the worth of business travel and business is very aware of its cost.

My friend Joe Segal, who is President of Kingswood Capital Corporation, a multi-million dollar operation that among other things, owns Mr. Jax Fashions, requires his buyers to travel frequently from their Vancouver home base to Toronto and Montreal on week-long buying trips.

No matter what you hear elsewhere, going on the road and living in hotels, eating in restaurants, stressing around in cabs, being constantly 'on' in an unfamiliar environment, is no fun.

How does Joe take advantage of all of this? He sends people off on their road trips Economy Class when they're fresh and ready for the tough road ahead.

Then when the deals are done and it's homeward bound, Joe's people fly First Class. It may be a carrot that rewards performance, but it works.

And boy, do those stretch-out seats and all that service ever feel good!

CHAPTER 10

The Man at the Palace

AS PART OF ITS CONTINUING ENTERTAINMENT franchise, TV Week Magazine in Vancouver talks often to the rich and famous, those fascinating people that we all love to read about, the people whose stories spice up our lives.

At the magazine, we approach these people in a number of different ways — through entertainment agencies who are anxious to promote upcoming television specials, through direct contact, through our own initiative to present a 'scoop' or a cover story that will help to generate sales.

One of the biggest T.V. events of the last quarter century was the marriage of Prince Charles and Princess Diana, something we knew was important, something that TV Week could splash in the biggest way. And being a royals groupie, I had every desire to be in the middle of the story.

To get a new slant on the upcoming event, my wife and I went to London with British Airways and through a number of channels, organized ourselves into a meeting not with the Queen, but certainly with her Secretary, a meeting that was to take place deep inside Buckingham Palace.

I should tell you that this is another of those stories where everything doesn't necessarily go right, that no matter how 'cool' we sometimes think we are, others can quite easily slip into power positions and turn us to jelly.

Kay and I were pretty nervous about going into the 'Buck,' as many Londoners call it. People crowd to its fences, but behind that fence is a place that has the power to intimidate the strongest among us.

Ready for the meeting, we trotted out for new clothes, for haircuts and hairdos, for manicures — everything one presumes one needs for a visit of this kind. We got ourselves a cab and said to the driver: "To the palace!" and he said: "Right guv," and away we went.

He stopped at the gate, and we said go on through and the bobby at the gate said: "Mr. and Mrs. Legge?" And we said yes and he waved us on. And at 2:59 p.m. precisely, we ended up at the West Wing entrance, were met by a page and ushered into Buckingham Palace.

Well, for a kid from the other side of London, it was spectacular. All the marble, all the gilt-edged finery, all the paintings, the busts, the blinding extravagance. Familiar faces from Henry VIII onward peered back at us as we squeaked along 300 yards of palace corridor in our new shoes to the room where we would spend 20 minutes in an interview with the secretary to the Queen.

We met, and for the next 10 minutes or so, he answered — without too much emotion or enthusiasm — the questions that would help fill the pages of our publication. He really wasn't friendly and not only did I feel intimidated, I felt singularly unwelcome. And if I include Kay, doubly unwelcome.

With 10 minutes to go and no more questions, I uncorked my rapier wit. There was no malice intended. It's just that the occasion and the moment had turned me into an imbecile.

"Tell me," I said, gesturing at the yards of art that hung from the walls, "are these originals?"

The gentleman looked pained. "Mr. Legge," he said, with due pomp, "EVERYthing in this palace is an original."

I pushed on.

"You, sir, must have the most interesting P.R. job in the world. How on earth do you GET a job like this?"

"One thing you don't do," he said, "is apply for it."

"No," I said, "you certainly wouldn't do that."

And we left.

The magazine we produced on Chuck and Di was spectacularly successful. But in retrospect it probably would have been JUST as successful if we had waited for the press releases and not worried about the man at the palace.

CHAPTER 11

Give a Little, Get a Lot

THE DEAD SEA IS DEAD because water flows INTO it, but nothing flows OUT of it. Bracken, stagnant, it is a gigantic collecting point where everything comes to a salty stop.

The Sea of Galilee, in the same part of the world, is alive. Water comes in and water goes out. It is cleansed, aerated and supporting of life — of fish, of birds, of people who are much more interested in the environment of that sea.

People are something like these two bodies of water. We can cause things — often it's money — to flow into our lives. And we can build fortunes and bless ourselves with all the trappings of what we believe wealth is all about. But we don't necessarily enrich ourselves in ways that bring the richest kind of satisfaction.

We end up like King Midas who lost himself in a jackpot with his wish for gold. We end up like the Dead

Sea, stagnant in many respects, salty and crusty round the edges.

Life can be enriched when wealth flows in and wealth and talent flows out.

All my life I have attempted to save 10% of everything I make for the life I hope I can live tomorrow. We all need financial security and that's why I would recommend that the saving habit start as soon as possible for each of us.

With equal dedication, I have attempted to give away 10% of everything I make.

It may sound like a lot, but I have discovered time and time again that this action has never failed to bless me richly in all kinds of tangible ways.

Like the Sea of Galilee, we can take it in, but we are made that much better when it flows through.

It's an action that's the stuff of life.

CHAPTER 12

Frank Rethinks Life

SOMETHING WE LEARN as we grow older, and hopefully wiser, is that most everything changes. It happens in business, it happens in life, where others have talked about the 'passages' we go through, where the people we were yesterday are not the people we are today.

Change is why something like marriage is such a constant challenge, why those who have chosen to share that incredible human relationship must try always to openly share the nuances of change — and respect that it happens.

At 40, 50 or whatever, we are NOT the innocents we were when we walked down the aisle at 20 or 30. It takes a ton of love and understanding to keep things rolling the way we always hoped they would!

My friend Frank Palmer is Chairman and Chief Executive Officer of Palmer Jarvis Advertising, a Vancouver company that in 1991 will have billings edging up towards $100 million, making it one of the biggest ad agencies in Canada. Over the years Frank has done some powerful work for a lot of people inside and outside of business.

A few years ago, Frank ran an ad on behalf of his company that expressed what he then thought about what makes a Palmer Jarvis partner. In fact that was the headline on the ad — What Makes a Palmer Jarvis Partner. It was pretty tough stuff and these are the points he listed:

The years without a holiday.

Late nights in the office when your contemporaries were in the pub.

Putting it back into the business when everyone was taking it out.

The school sports days you never saw.

The friendships you had to leave behind.

Paying a bonus to everyone except yourself.

Backing your hunch — with your home.

Risking your health for the health of the business.

Remembering everyone who helped you on your way.

Forgiving those who didn't.

Refusing to give up when the finances ran down.

Not leaving the bridge when things got rough.

Keeping your nerve when all around were losing their shirts.

Missing your children's first steps into the world.

Handicapping your golf instead of your business.

Dropping out of university to do your own thing. And actually doing it.

Demanding excellence in everything you do.

And a lot more than most are prepared to give.

Do things change? In permitting me to use the words of his ad, Frank says that, in retrospect, several items in the ad no longer apply. I didn't ask which ones.

But as I was going to press with this book, I was flipping through a recent media publication and I saw another Palmer Jarvis ad, signed by Frank.

It said simply: "We respect the power of change. We've learned how to deal with it positively and we're turning it into success for our clients." That was it.

I'm glad he said that, and I'm even happier that Frank appears to have shifted his priorities.

I just hate the thought of someone missing their children's first steps, not to mention some regular rounds of golf.

CHAPTER 13

Life is for the Future

I DO A LOT OF TRAVELLING and I buy a lot of books. Mostly books of wisdom, the kind that are always available at airports — the thoughts of others that I can consume and appreciate in the quiet miles of the sky.

Sometimes the books I have heard about aren't readily available. They go out of print, end up in regional circulation, or simply disappear.

Last summer, my wife and I went on a bus tour through parts of England that I hadn't seen for years and on one sunny afternoon we ended up outside a bookstore called Blackwell's in the university city of Oxford.

"This store, ladies and gentlemen," said the driver, "has any book you want."

That's quite a boast. But knowing what I wanted and couldn't get elsewhere, and knowing quite a bit about the reputation of British bookstores, I walked into Blackwell's and said to the clerk at the counter: "Do you have Victor Frankl's book, Man's Search for Meaning?"

He clicked away for a few moments on a computer, then directed me to another clerk on a computer and eventually to a bookshelf that contained six copies of Man's Search for Meaning. I bought all of them. With several floors, each 10,000 square feet in area, book-bountiful Blackwell's had come through in style.

All of which is a rather long introduction to a book that I love. If you can find it, I suggest you add it to your own collection of volumes of great wisdom. Hodder and Stoughton in Toronto may be able to help.

Man's Search for Meaning was published in Austria in 1946 and was translated into English in 1953. Dr. Frankl spent three years as a prisoner in four different concentration camps and learned about every conceivable extreme of human suffering. But he used his experiences to find ways of healing sickness of the mind and spirit. His belief is that man has amazing powers of endurance so long as it makes sense to him to go on living.

"He who has a why to live can bear with any how," says Frankl.

On one occasion, after he had been persistently beaten, as he froze, after he had watched friends and family die beside him, as he was forced to march to work and dig in icy ditches, Frankl wrote: "Occasionally I looked at the sky, where the stars were fading and the pink light of the morning was beginning to spread behind a dark bank of clouds. But my mind clung to my wife's image, imagining it with an uncanny acuteness. I heard her answering me, saw her smile, her frank and encouraging look. Real or not, her look was then more luminous than the sun which was beginning to rise.

"A thought transfixed me: for the first time in my life I saw the truth as it is set into song by so many poets, proclaimed as the final wisdom by so many thinkers. The truth — that love is the ultimate and the highest goal to which man can aspire. Then I grasped the meaning of the greatest secret that human poetry and human thought and belief have to impart: The salvation of man is through love and in love . . ."

" . . . In a last violent protest against the hopelessness of imminent death, I sensed my spirit piercing through the enveloping gloom. I felt it transcend that hopeless, meaningless world, and from somewhere I heard a victorious "Yes" in answer to my question of the existence of an ultimate purpose."

Ever since my visit to Blackwell's in Oxford, I have been blessed by the hope that Frankl expressed again and again.

Everything CAN be taken from us, but NOT the last human freedom — the freedom to choose our attitude in any given set of circumstances, to choose our own way.

Life is always for the future.

CHAPTER 14

What are *You* Hiding?

PHANTOM OF THE OPERA is an incredible work that has touched the heart of the world. I have seen it in London, New York and Toronto and I will see it again in Vancouver. The simplicity of the story, the *power* of the story, draws me back, draws others back. No matter where it is staged, there is an understanding of the Phantom's magic.

At the heart of this story is the mask that hides the phantom's disfigured face. It is a powerful image. It is a camouflaging wall to what lies behind it.

For the Phantom, the mask is protection not just of his face, but of almost everything about him. For the most part he hides behind it very well. But the story evolves and Christine's kiss not only removes the mask, but gives the Phantom recognition, shows him love.

Andrew Lloyd Webber, the brilliant British musician who wrote Phantom, says that he believes the story is an expression of the isolation that people feel. It doesn't matter who we are, there is always something about ourselves that we want to change, or perhaps hide.

All of this interpretation — by the man who wrote the show and from us who have seen it and applaud its world success — is clear indication that we can relate to the message of loneliness, that we ALL at some time or another hide behind masks.

Let me share with you some thoughts that are titled Hear What I'm NOT Saying. I believe it's right on the topic of what we all, from time to time, feel:

Don't be fooled by me.

Don't be fooled by the face I wear.

For I wear a mask, I wear a thousands masks, masks that I'm afraid to take off, and none of them is me.

Pretending is an art that is second nature to me, but don't be fooled.

I give the impression that I'm secure, that all is sunny and unruffled with me, within as well as without, that confidence is my name and coolness is my game — that the water is calm and I'm in command, and that I need no one. But don't believe me.

Please.

My surface may be smooth, but my surface is my mask.

Beneath lies no smugness, no complacency.

Beneath dwells the real me in confusion, in fear, in aloneness.

But I hide this. I don't want anybody to know it.

I panic at the thought of my weakness and fear being exposed.

66

That's why I frantically create a mask to hide behind, a nonchalant, sophisticated facade, to help me pretend, to shield me from the glance that knows.

But such a glance is precisely my salvation.

My only salvation. And I know it.

That is, if it is followed by acceptance.

It's the only thing that can liberate me from myself, from my own self-built prison walls, from the barriers that I painstakingly erect.

It's the only thing that will assure me of what I can't assure myself, that I'm really worth something. But I don't tell you this.

I'm afraid your glance will not be followed by acceptance and love.

I'm afraid you'll think less of me, that you'll laugh, and your laugh will wound me.

I'm afraid that deep down, I'm not much, and you will see this and reject me.

So I play my game, my pretending game, behind a facade of assurance.

So when I'm going through my routine, do not be fooled by what I'm saying.

Please listen, listen carefully, and try to hear what I'm not saying, what I'd like to be able to say, but can't.

Who I am, you may wonder.

I am someone you know very well,

Every man and every woman you will ever meet.

CHAPTER 15

Taking on Goliath

WE'VE ALL MADE DEALS in our lives. And by deals I don't mean transactions that in any way harmed anyone. I mean transactions that others describe as win-win, a price that's right for everyone.

Jim Pattison is a Vancouver businessman with a formidable reputation, and a business empire worth hundreds of millions. The public knows Jimmy through real and imagined legends. A car dealer who each month fires the person or persons at the bottom of the sales list. A guy who would move in, accumulate stock and take majority interest in the largest companies and boggle the minds of the big markets. The financier who flies every weekend by private jet from Vancouver to Switzerland to do deals and count his money in numbered bank accounts. The trumpet player who goes to church every Sunday and annually leaves one tenth of his earnings in the collection plate. The man who was asked to run

EXPO 86 in Vancouver and pulled off what is generally recognized as one of the best shows in grand scale exposition history — that changed forever the way Vancouver looks at itself and is looked at by the world community. Jimmy is a remarkable guy.

One of the things that Jimmy did along the way was get into the publishing business. For whatever reason, a lot of people dabble in or get serious about publishing. Some have done very well. But for the unsuspecting, it can be a minefield of surprises.

Being in the business myself, I had made approaches a few years back to acquire a couple of well known business magazines in Vancouver to add to the solid stable we already owned. But the deal fell through and life went on.

Then Jimmy moved in, and successfully acquired one of the publications we had been chasing — and three similar publications in Western Canada.

In the months that followed, we watched them closely and learned that perhaps all was not well in the new division of Jimmy's publishing enterprise.

So I phoned, suggesting that a sale might make things more comfortable for the Pattison Group, and was offered a price of $2.5 million.

I knew immediately that it was high, but I was wise enough to say that if all things checked out in the due diligence report that would follow, I could accept the price.

After a decent interval, very much aware of Jimmy's reputation as a killer deal maker, I called back with a counter offer of $1 million, payable over time, interest free.

If I may use poetic licence, they laughed in my face. But I sensed that all was not lost and 10 days later, they called again saying that an alternate offer had fallen through and they were again interested.

With incredible support throughout all of this from my executive assistant Karen Foss and bravado that somehow won the day, we purchased four magazines for $800,000, paid back over four years, interest free.

Jimmy was off an uncomfortable hook and we added to business that we knew, business that could be comfortably assimilated into our existing company.

Observers looked at the deal, which got a lot of publicity in the business press, as a kind of David and Goliath thing and, all things considered, I was very proud that we had been able to pull it off.

But if there's a bigger message, it's probably that the fear and trembling we feel in life is often quite unjustified.

In our case, Jimmy wanted to unload something that was unfamiliar to him, we wanted it, and somewhere in the middle was a price that was comfortable for both of us. His imagined reputation had absolutely nothing to do with it.

The uncertainty that comes when we think about meeting bankers, going to dentists, all of the other things we often dread, has mostly nothing to do with reality. Bankers are bad, but not THAT bad, and dentistry has come a long way in recent years!

Don't think about the road to success, think about what's at the end of the road.

I'm not suggesting the same drastic measures, but that old villian Lady Macbeth had it right when she coaxed her wavering husband into action: "Screw your courage to the sticking place," she said, "and we'll not fail."

Unfortunately for King Duncan, Macbeth certainly got the message.

When opportunity comes and you believe what you are about to do will succeed, there really is no alternative.

Just do it.

CHAPTER 16

Eppich Proportion

EBCO IS ONE OF THOSE COMPANIES that is so good it makes you ache.

It moves, it shakes, it grows. But more than anything, it cares, and through its actions, it teaches us powerful lessons for business and for life.

You may not have heard of Ebco. It got its start in British Columbia in 1956 in the tool and die business and ended its first year with sales of $10,000.

In 1991, making tools, dies and a whole lot more, they're projecting sales in excess of $124 million.

The company is run, driven and nurtured by twin brothers Hugo and Helmut Eppich. They look like the guy from the Love Boat. And love seems very much part of the way they make business and life unfold.

In 1990 B.C. Business Magazine named the Eppichs Entrepreneurs of the Year and in her perspective on the couple, Patti Schom-Moffatt wrote:

"For many entrepreneurs corporate growth and success come at the expense of the informal ways they carried on business in the past — the time spent chatting with employees, the pride in workmanship, the fun and satisfaction of doing rather than managing. All too often, entrepreneurs-gone-corporate can lose touch with the very ideals that drove them into running their own show in the first place.

"Hugo and Helmut Eppich are proof that it doesn't have to happen that way. Rather than abandon their value system . . . they enshrined it. And as it turns out, the value system — the importance they place on people, perfection and prosperity, in that order — has provided just the kind of solid foundation a large, successful corporation requires to survive."

Ebco today is into aerospace and furniture manufacturing, land development, computer software, high tech farming — not to mention tool and die making and metal finishing. Their plants are dotted around the B.C. Lower Mainland and Alberta. Their head office and key manufacturing property is smack in the middle of Richmond, Vancouver's populous southern suburb.

Lots of companies talk about corporate values, and some even practice them. At Ebco, the values have been written down, printed and circulated, and every day in dozens of tangible ways are part of what's happening within this amazing company.

Ebco's corporate values build a pyramid of meaning. Three principal components — of person, perfection and prosperity — break into three more principal sections. The person into love, dignity and respect. Perfection into excellence, virtue and merit. Prosperity into health, wealth and happiness.

Another 10 sub-divisions add further meaning.

Love means to be caring, sharing, helping, understanding, charitable, harmonizing, trusting, honest, praising and dedicated.

Dignity means to be valued, virtuous, prosperous, decent, achieving, communicating, free enterprise, secure, honoured, prestigious.

Respect means respect for the individual's ethnic background, cultural background, religious background, racial background, gender, opinion. It means to be considerate, be fair, be courteous, listen.

Under the perfection heading, excellence means achieving excellence in quality, service, value, productivity, thriftiness, leadership, creativity, innovation, education, communication.

Practicing the virtues means prudence, justice, fortitude, moderation, faith, hope, charity, entrepreneurship, internationalism, action.

Corporate merit is gained through righteousness, integrity, peace and harmony, loyalty and duty, vision, mission, persistence, success, cooperation, safety.

Prosperity? Corporate health is maintained and balanced with corporate values, strategies and goals, finances, lifelong learning, internal and external communications, internal and external changes, global advisors and board members, socioethic activities, the upgrading of capital assets, simplicity.

Corporate wealth is maintained with superior return on investment, market share, revenue growth, workforce and facilities, products and services, suppliers, sources of wisdom, global learning and networking, independent asset pools, corporate successors.

Corporate happiness is attained and maintained by keeping active and busy, planning and setting goals, productivity. It means being positive, being yourself, being sociable, eliminating negative feelings, trying not to worry, valuing close relationships, living for today and expressing your happiness.

All of these values have tangible results — corporate and personal gifts to the local food bank; the raising of $1.6 million to sponsor a University Chair in Expert Systems; the receiving of a Race Relations Award from the Government of Canada; the design and building of a Cyclotron at the University of B.C.; the receiving of Boeing's prestigious Eagle Award for outstanding cost reduction and quality; a dramatic reduction in the accident rate to below industry average. Ebco has accumulated awards for individuals and groups of individuals — rich trophies coded with the words that are their values.

They respect six different religious holidays, from Christmas to Chinese New Year to the Muslim festival that ends Ramadan. They conduct an annual multicultural food festival.

"We have found that by focusing on the strengths rather than the differences of each culture, we all benefit," says Hugo Eppich.

And that's how twin brothers, who like to tinker, tuned a company to incredible heights of achievement and why British Columbians marvel at their example.

As I said earlier, it's all so good it makes you ache.

CHAPTER 17

Don't Judge a Cockney

I REMEMBER A STORY about a group of four good friends who graduated at the same time from Eton. It was a time of happiness and certain sadness. They knew that from that day on each would head off into different world directions, into careers that could quite likely split them up for long periods of time, perhaps forever.

"We're going to change over the years," said one of them. "We need a way to show each other who we are, to avoid any embarrassment when we meet."

"Right," said another. "Let's always keep the bottom button of our waistcoats undone. If we should meet, there will be immediate recognition." And they parted.

Many years later, bottom button undone, one of the four was walking in London and saw a very portly gentleman coming towards him and he too had his bottom waistcoat button undone.

It was his chance. "From Eton?" asked the first

man, pointing to the undone button.

"No," said the other looking down. "From drinkin."

I DO apologize. It's an awful way of getting into my second story, which is a whole lot better.

A friend of mine, who has the recognizable voice inflection of a grad from Eton or any of the other veddy British schools, told me about meeting a gentleman while flying First Class across Canada who not only was not an Eton grad but, perish the thought, a Cockney!

It was one of those familiar cases of class snobbery that still exists among the Brits. How can some poor blighter born within the sound of the Bow Bells be travelling First Class?

On the Cockney gentleman's lapel, however, was a pin sporting the highly respectable logo of the Rolls Royce Motor Company. Being seat companions for the long flight, the two of them got talking and the result of that conversation eventually led me to meet and to interview in Toronto the man who had worn the pin.

He told me he had come to Canada from London in 1956 with $50 in his pocket. Until then, it had been one of those lives that drift in and out of misadventure — the kind of searching we all do to find that one, clear, straight road.

"I left school, as all Cockneys do, at 14," he said, "to start work or steal or whatever one has to do to survive. You learn a lot in the streets of London."

He told me he had served in the Norwegian Merchant Navy, in the British National Service, and, because of his natural belligerence — his words — in the military police with a stint in Korea.

About then, he came to the realization that you

CAN make choices about life, as he would about his own. He could lead it forever as a petty larcenist, a continuation of his earlier days of street survival, or he could live and work within the law and make new and different things happen.

He came to Canada and fell in love with the country.

Life here as a young man fresh from army national service, was one of delivering bread, working on an assembly line building cash registers — and yearning to race motor cars and get rich quick.

So he set his sights on motor racing. It was a move made on a Friday. He remembers it, because he asked for the day off as he worked the cash register production line. The foreman said no.

"So I looked at all the people there and I thought, do I want to spend the next 20 years of my life here just to get a pension? I said to the foreman: who's the next guy to be laid off? And he said, that chap over there. And I said: tell him he's got my job. And I left."

He had the drive, but at that stage no car.

But there was an ad in the paper that day, looking for men to run an auto business. Along with '482 million' other people, he applied. Foregoing the promised salary, commission, fringe benefits and demonstrator, he and six others got the job. With help from manager John Hayden — and a gift of the gab picked up on the streets of London — he became a salesman and got himself into the automobile business.

He never did become a champion race driver, but he did find wealth and a career far removed from the streets of London.

With his partners, John Cox would ultimately own

a company called Rolls Royce on Bay Street in downtown Toronto. The busiest corner in Toronto and no doubt the busiest corner in Canada. His company would sell Rolls Royce, Bentleys, Jaguars, Rovers and other fine cars. And, because they needed the parts to service sales of the 16 Aston Martins they had in stock, they would, in due course, own the company that made them.

Today, John Cox sells 59% of all the Rolls Royce cars sold in Canada. John gave me his four "Driving" rules for success:

1. Believe in yourself – totally.
2. Do what you know and understand.
3. Be committed – from the inside.
4. Be willing to gamble on you own judgement.

Dialects — and the world is packed with them — are never indicative of who we really are. They are part of the makeup of each of us.

Like John, we can start anywhere, make life decisions, head straight for the top.

"If I'm going to believe, really believe then I've got to risk it all."

John Cox can be recognized today not by an undone button on his waistcoat, but by the double R's of Rolls Royce in his lapel — and a dialect that despite the passage of years, identifies him as a true blue Londoner.

Just like me.

CHAPTER 18

Service with a Shine

THIS IS A STORY that for the longest time had a beginning and a middle, but no definitive ending. For a long time, I used to tell the incomplete story. But with an ending, it became much better.

A couple of years ago, I was asked to be the master of ceremonies for a very posh event that had sold out the ballroom of a large Vancouver hotel. More than 1,000 people would be there. They expected the best.

What would I wear? It's not a question one has to ask too often, but when it comes to presentation, there is always a choice. In this case, there was no doubt at all that I would be wearing a tuxedo. It went with the evening — a dash of fashion formality that inevitably adds a little extra when the occasional is special.

I have a tux and all of the trimmings, but I hadn't worn it for some time and when I checked on the day of the event, I discovered that I had no matching black shoes — absolutely nothing in the way of footwear to match the elegance of the tuxedo. Sandals, sneakers and battered brown brogues, but nothing in complementary black.

But there was still time to fix the problem and during the course of my business day, I walked into a very prominent shoe store in downtown Vancouver and told the clerk, who on that occasion also happened to be the manager, of my predicament.

"No problem," he said, as he started measuring my foot, "we'll get you squared away in no time."

You should know that the name of the company was and is Sheppard Shoes — a retailer of considerable reputation in Vancouver. The name is important to the story. I will also let you know that the quoted price on the shoes being offered me that day was $350! For a pair of shoes, it seemed like a fortune, but being frantic or perhaps a bit foolish, I O.K.'d the price.

I was making progress. The bad news was the price. But the good news was that I could get the shoes I wanted to go with the tuxedo. Everything would work out.

Except that there was more bad news. I learned moments later that the shoes I wanted weren't in stock at that store, but — more good news! — they were in stock at Sheppard's second store several blocks away, where, it was suggested, I could go to pick them up.

Your expectations in life may be different from mine, but when I heard that bit of news from the man at Sheppard's, I was very disappointed. Having just said yes to a $350 pair of shoes, and having expressed concern about the limits on my time, I figured that maybe Sheppard's might offer to have one of their people bring the shoes to me. The way I looked at it, that's what service is all about.

Not to mention the potential benefits to the Sheppard people. While the shoes were on their way, wasn't this an opportunity to offer me additional merchandise? I was already identified as a mark! More shoes, laces, socks, polish, even the store? And didn't anyone think that once I'd left that store on the long trek to the second store, maybe another store that sold shoes might catch my eye? Net result? Lost sale, and an upset customer who would go about life spreading the bad word.

I didn't get upset or make demands. I walked to the second store, paid my $350, and was a smash hit at the big dinner.

But I began to tell the shoe story in subsequent speaking engagements. I told thousands of people about those shoes and what I perceived as less than great service in that transaction.

It was a cycle that may never have ended, except that one day, the third part of the story was sitting right in one of those audiences. It was the man who ran Sheppard Shoes.

Of course he was upset. But he wanted desperately to make amends. He told me that he would follow up on my complaint, that in future there would be a clear understanding by the Sheppard people about service, about pampering customers, about the importance of setting and meeting standards of customer satisfaction. That, he said, was a guarantee!

He was as good as his word. No one was fired, because it didn't require that kind of action. But the message was clear and the personal followup was as much and more than I could have expected.

And that was almost the ending of the story.

He only asked that if I ever told the story again, could I please add that he and the Sheppard people had corrected the situation, that the story had a happy ending?

I said I would, and I have.

Every customer in the world, buying everything from shoes to ships to sealing wax, has an expectation of service. And even though standards of service should always be uniformly high, it's human nature for us to expect more service when we're spending more money.

Most of the time when service is bad, we don't tell the person who served us. We just don't come back, and what's worse for the person or company that served us, is that we keep telling and telling that story of bad service. And those we tell, tell others, and in due course hundreds and thousands of people hear about it. And in every re-telling, it gets worse!

You never know about customers. That's why we must always respect them for the heaven-sent treasures they are. It is that unique one-on-one relationship, no matter what you do, that will, at very least, maintain your business, and at most — more good news! — build your business.

I have walked many miles in my black shoes. They were ridiculously expensive, but they are also shoes of great quality and superb comfort.

I thank the Sheppard people for finding them for me — and for giving me the beginning, the middle and the ending to a nice story.

CHAPTER 19

What Are You Building?

A tourist walked up to a couple of London bricklayers
who were building a wall with considerable care.
"So, my good man," he said to the first, "and what are
YOU doing?"
"Buildin' a wall," he said. "I'm a bricklayer."
"And you?" he asked the second man. "What about
YOU?"
"Me?" he answered. "I'm buildin' a cathedral to the
glory of God. STRONG it will be. And TRUE. An'
its bricks and mortar will last for a hundred
generations."
"Well that's pretty stupid, mate," said the first
bricklayer, continuing to slap on the mortar.
"You're supposed to be buildin' a garage."

The joke went SOMETHING like that. But maybe it should have stopped before the punchline. The nice part about the story is that the second bricklayer did his job with obvious purpose. He knew that whatever he was doing, it was integral to the whole job, something bigger than mere bricks, even if he WAS a bit off track.

In the show Working, adapted from Studs Terkel's great book about the everyday jobs of everyday people, there's a marvellous song about those who build skyscrapers.

From the dreams of builders, the money of banks, the plans of architects, it always comes down to, or it's really UP to the steel men, the bricklayers, the glaziers, the painters — the army of men and women who REAL-LY make buildings, bridges and cathedrals. THEY know what they're doing and they do it well. Like bricklayer No. 2, the project must become much more than themselves.

It's what pride is all about. We do so many things that don't seem to add up to a hill of beans — and often they don't. But sometimes they do. All we have to do is click in to the fact that collectively we can do great things, that the whole is made up of the parts that are you and me.

We can lay bricks or we can build cathedrals.

CHAPTER 20

How's Your Memory?

IT'S IMPORTANT TO SAY PLEASE and thank you. And it's important to remember the names of people.

It is our name that gives each of us a special identity. Sometimes we may not be crazy about the seemingly dreadful choice that was made for us by our parents, but most of the time, we are proud to be who we are, to be called what we are.

And we like others to call us by our name. It's a mark of recognition that's appreciated. When a hotel clerk or a restaurant host says welcome and calls us by name, we warm immediately to the moment, look differently at that caring person, and at his or her surroundings. We feel good.

Too often, when someone says: "Bill, I would like you to meet Barbara," we say hi, shake hands and immediately forget Barbara's name. And all Barbara gets from us in future exchanges is a grunt. Barbara, after a brief moment of recognition, returns again to the lonely world of anonymity.

Bill Clennan calls himself Mr. Memory. Up to 250 times a year, he speaks to audiences around the world about the importance of remembering the names of people. He is a master of memory and his audiences are inspired by his message — his ability to load up his memory with name after name of the people he meets.

I don't have Bill's memory secrets, but I try to remember that names are important — that we can and should switch on our incredible brains when someone says: "Bill, I would like you to meet Barbara." "Hi Barbara. Nice to meet you." "Hi Bill. Nice to meet YOU."

Our memory works when it's important to us to make it work. Our memory works when we take that special moment to enter new data and to store it, to be retrieved at any future time to make business work, to make someone feel better because they have been recognized by the name that is their very own.

During one of our meetings, Bill Clennan gave me some words that he wrote. Not the complete secret of his memory success, but perhaps a philosophy that helps him perform memory miracles. I asked if I could share it and he said, certainly.

> The contest lasts for moments
> Though the training's taken years
> It wasn't the winning alone that
> was worth the work and the tears
> The applause will be forgotten
> The prize will be misplaced
> But the long hard hours of practice

Will never be a waste
For in trying to win
You build a skill
You learn that winning
Depends on will
You never grow by how much you win
You only grow by how much you put in
So any new challenge
You've just begun
Put forth your best
And you've already won.

"Hi, Barbara. Nice to see you again."

CHAPTER 21

10 Ways to Help You Soar

IN MY LIFE THERE ARE 10 PRINCIPLES, rules, points — call them what you will — that help me to soar with the eagles.

There may be others, but for me these guideposts focus on the Big Things — and besides, if you load yourself with too much to remember, you start to forget.

Each time I speak to a group of people, I finish with these 10 points. You may wish to include them in YOUR life. The importance you attach to any one is not important. What IS important is the collective benefit these principles will add to your success, and even more importantly, to your happiness.

Determination

Persistence. It' O.K. to fail. You WILL fail. The moment you begin making decisions you will fail. But you don't stop when you fail. You pick yourself up, dust yourself off and start making MORE decisions that this time are supported by the wisdom that rubbed off from your last failure. General Colin Powell, Chairman of the U.S. Joint Chiefs of Staff, the brilliant strategist at the heart of the allied victory against Iraq, says that success is the result of perfection, hard work and learning from failure. Maybe Vietnam was the mistake that gave the U.S. the wisdom and the determination to win in the Gulf. Begin, and keep on going.

Honesty

Always speak and live the truth, no ifs, ands, buts or maybes. It's a sad commentary on the North American business society when an organization like the Harvard Business School has to put millions of dollars into a Business Ethics department to focus on white collar crime! Be honest, with everyone.

Responsibility

Be trustworthy, be dependable. Isn't that what you want people to think of you? Someone others can count on? I think this of the people who work for me. I can say that no matter where I go, I can count on them. They're dependable. They won't let me down.

Thoughtfulness

Think of others before yourself. It's the toughest thing you may ever do, but once you start it becomes easier every time. And while your actions should never be motivated by what's in it for you, the benefits of your actions will come rolling in. If we go through life serving others, encouraging others, seeing extraordinary things in ordinary things, being thoughtful in the way we deal with those around us who are 85% of the reason for our success, we will succeed, we will be remembered.

Confidentiality
Respect it. Don't share information that you've been asked to keep to yourself. Absorb it, store it and get on with your life.

Punctuality
A big thing? You bet it is. Be on time. Every time. You wouldn't believe how much it adds to your credibility.

Self Control
We get caught up with our own emotions and make wrong decisions. Count to ten — or whatever it takes — to make you pause for a moment and be objective. Make decisions, but make them with wisdom. Sleep on it. Things often look different in the morning.

Patience
There is always a time of waiting. Be willing to wait in all of those situations where impatience often takes hold. You will have to wait to own your own business, to become president, to reach any number of personal goals. You will require patience to hear the other person out. Be patient. Your turn will come.

Purity

Reject anything that lowers your personal standards or the standards of those you serve. You know what's right, what's expected of you within a corporation. There's really only one way to go. Make that choice and keep on making it. You will hold your head high.

Compassion

When someone else hurts, feel that hurt with them. You can always turn away and leave compassion to others — or you can draw close and give the love and caring that IS inside you. You would expect no less. To offer compassion is always one of life's rich experiences. Be the Good Samaritan.

CHAPTER 22

Bamboo Wisdom

THE BAMBOO OF CHINA is one of the world's most fascinating bits of flora.

It is used for scaffolding in the building of sky-scrapers, as a conduit for irrigation, in the crafting of furniture, household goods and countless artifacts. Like rice or chopsticks or M.S.G., it's one of the many great mysteries of the mysterious East.

But perhaps the biggest fascination about the bamboo of China is the nature of its growth.

Before you ever see the first missile-shaped sprout of the bamboo, it lies underground as an undeveloped plant. Not just for a year must the bamboo be nurtured. Nor two, or three. But four. It takes four years to bring a bamboo to visible life.

Then in the fifth year it explodes into being. Overnight, a dewy, sap-soaked black sprout pushes from its earthen prison and in just one day it grows a foot, sometimes more.

Then the next day, with all these years of nurturing behind it, it adds another foot, then another and another, until it reaches a height of almost 100 feet in almost as many days. Spectacular!

I like the bamboo and I like the way it comes into being.

From the bamboo, I see a clear manifestation of the way nature handles its growth.

And more? If you want something spectacular, you have to work at it. The miracles come, but there are dues to pay.

Kids, employees, careers — you plant seeds and the watering is your wisdom, the fertilizing is your patience and understanding.

Then one day, when you least expect it, that kid, that employee, that career will bloom and there will be no turning back.

Think about the bamboo of China.

Expect the unexpected.

CHAPTER 23

Teeing up for Life

ONLY IN RECENT TIMES have I begun to get the hang of golf.

Over the years, others would say: "There's nothing more relaxing than a game of golf." I would say: "There's nothing more frustrating, intimidating or demeaning."

For some, golf relieves stress. To hear the satisfying click that sends the ball off into the stratospheric distance; to watch the ball leap from the sand and bite the green six inches or better from the pin; to putt, and watch the ball roll with seeming confidence to a rattling end in the cup — all of these are satisfactions, indeed.

Unless you don't know how. In which case it can be a hapless adventure in hooks, slices, whiffs, chops, flying divots, sand and atrocious language.

Red Poling, who at this writing is chairman of Ford and a golfer with an eight handicap, says that his office game parallels his golf game.

Says Red: "The three most important things in business and in golf are consistency, dependability and predictability. If my game is good, it's because I'm consistent in my swing. I don't need a big wide fairway."

Jay Hall, a management consultant in Houston wrote a book called The Executive Trap in which he talks about a personal theory that there's a correlation between the way we perform on the job and the way we play golf.

"In its construction, golf is the one game that most nearly parallels human life experience," Hall says.

Nothing duplicates the subtle nuances, exhilaration and bad breaks of life as well as the game of golf. And nothing, says Hall, poses a bigger dilemma to executives on the course and in the office than their ambivalence about making decisions.

"We've got an epidemic of flawed executive leadership," he says. "These executives either don't know how to make a decision or, once they do, are afraid to make it for fear that once they do, they'll have to give up something else that is important to them."

In the case of Ford's Poling, it is not as much a matter of decision making as playing strategically. He says he tries to imbue his management style with the same strong focus on strategy that he uses in golf.

"As you walk up to the next shot, you're not looking at the beautiful scenery around you. You're watching the terrain, noticing the impact of the wind, looking at the green, checking the hazards. Then, if you miss the shot, you're trying to see how it will affect the game."

He reaches for balance. "Everyone likes to hit a

drive the farthest, but you actually use a driver less than you do a putter."

And timing? "You must get the product to market on time. If you delay, you'll miss the whole market for that product. I learned about timing at a golf club in England where the requirement was that you had to be finished with your game in three hours or less. It showed me what you can do if you just concentrate."

Until recently, I wouldn't have understood these analogies that Mr. Hall and Mr. Poling are talking about. You need to work your way through the Wall of Golfing Frustration to find the beginnings of enjoyment on the other side.

But if I may continue mixing my metaphors, I think I may have done just that, learning that golf can be a fairway of fun, that its rewards come not just from the exhilaration of the game's surroundings, but in chipping away at the strokes one by one, reducing scores and increasing satisfaction.

Not too long ago, feeling particularly confident, and with the effrontery of any First Time Golfer, I challenged my coach to a round, suggesting that the winner buy dinner for four, provide a limousine for the evening and offer an open choice of wine for the occasion. He looked startled, but agreed.

I can only say that my bill was absolutely humungous — and despite the fact that we make progress, becoming a golf champion DOES take a little time.

Have YOU driven a ball, lately?

CHAPTER 24

31,000 Days!

ON AVERAGE, IF WE'RE CAREFUL, we Westerners live to be about 85 years old. For a tree that might be maturity. For us, it's often senility!

How we're functioning at 85 depends on what we did during the intervening years. Work, exercise, stress — all of these things have a very direct effect on the old bod and the brain that's inside it.

Zig Ziglar tells a great story about his own quest to exercise. He often told his audiences that for him, exercise means filling the tub, jumping in, pulling the plug and fighting the current.

But back to my point. Eighty five years is just over a thousand months. Now do you feel a little more like a true mortal?

How about just 4,420 weeks? Try 31,000 days! That's a lifetime.

When people come up to me and say: "Have a nice

day!" I say thank you very much.

But with just 31,000 of them in my lifetime allotment, I need a lot more than simply 'nice.' I need GREAT!

And that's what I tell the people I meet. What's more, *I* take it a full 180 degrees from the passive to the active.

MAKE it a great day, is what I say. Take charge of what you're doing and *MAKE* it what you want it to be.

You could wait a lifetime for a nice day to land on you.

But a great day that you make yourself?

It's yours for the making.

CHAPTER 25

Learning Louie Lore

THOSE OF YOU WHO ARE MATURE ENOUGH to remember the Sixties will remember, among other things, a piece of writing called Desiderata.

Printed on posters, quoted by everyone from so-called peaceniks to the occasional Canadian prime minister, Desiderata's gentle message was claimed to have been a resurrected piece of ancient philosophy that was unearthed in a church in Boston — if memory serves me correctly.

The true story about Desiderata is that it was quite new, written by one Max Elormann, a lawyer from Terre Haute, Indiana. Despite the campy reputation it subsequently attained, we loved Desiderata and each of us WAS a child of the universe who had a right to be heard.

All of which leads me not to a church in Boston or a lawyer's office in Indiana, but to a modern office in Vancouver. There I discovered another kind of special wisdom.

The firm of H.Y. Louie is large, well known and highly respected on Canada's west coast. It has been commercially linked with the Orient for many years and its enterprise, through the grocery trade and later into many other major retail endeavours, touches British Columbians in tens of thousands of everyday transactions.

I was in the offices of H.Y. Louie one afternoon and while waiting for my appointment, I couldn't help but see three framed letters hanging on the reception area wall.

They were written in the months of March, May and July in the year 1934 by Hok Yat Louie to his son Bill. Hok Yat — the H.Y. of the company — was in Hong Kong and his son was in Vancouver.

Like Desiderata, the letters were full of simple truths that at that time were intended as guiding rules for the new Louie business. But they were also rules for life. The Louie family was kind enough to let me copy the words for use in this book.

In his first letter, written on Canadian Pacific Steamship Lines stationery, Hok Yat said in part:

"Life is for the pursuit of happiness. Young people should always be earnest in their work. Treat your customers with trust and loyalty. Honour your mother, to your older brother show respect, to your younger brothers and sisters offer them good advice . . . that is what pursuit of happiness in life is all about. When pursuing prosperity you must follow the laws of heaven. Don't be afraid to be kind and charitable, ill deeds should be avoided. These are my words of advice for you to preserve and treasure and to remember."

In May, after expressing concern that he had not received a letter in the interim, Hok Yat wrote:

" . . . Now that you have spent time in a prestigious school, you should preserve your own reputation. Now that you are helping out in the business, you should assist in everything in the shop . . . You as the younger brother should help out in all matters and listen to (your brother's) instructions as the manager. Be earnest, fair and loyal in your dealings with customers. Discuss things with your fellow workers. Be amiable to them. Show respect to your mother so as not to forget her big task in bringing you up. Acquiesce to her wishes."

After receiving a reply from Bill, Hok Yat wrote his third letter from Hong Kong in July:

"I received your report on the progress of our business and your progress in learning the basics to the benefit of the family. We are father and son, brother with brother in the pursuit of a good living — expenses and expenditures should be planned as things progress. The execution of these plans is left to yourselves as long as you set your goals based on the business's profitability. It requires work and care not to step out of the focal point.

"Young people are always anxious, but their minds can be very simple. Under the present situation, your older brother Tim is the manager of the business. His authority encompasses all cash coming in and going out, buying and selling and all customer accounts . . . As brothers you should cohesively work together and assist when you can. Discuss problems with each other. The older brother is a friend and the younger brother must show respect. (I) hope you will remember this so that the business will remain stable.

"For a learner you must be prepared to spend nights to study and memorize what is taught. You can concentrate on the bookkeeping work. Do it with a clear head. The more you learn, the better you get. One precious lesson to learn is that you do not have to rely on others. You learn to be sharp. Develop your own character as well as your working skills.

"Always remember to honour your parents, especially your mother who has the task of bringing you up. By following their wishes you are honouring them."

For more than half a century Hok Yat's words have been a constant in the Louie family's success. Incredibly simple, completely understandable advice that came from a father who cared not just about business, but about the importance of family, of respect, of working and living together.

The H.Y. Louie company is valued beyond dollars and cents. Its real value lies in its people, culture, customer base, ethical business standards and more importantly how it is viewed by others. Even more encouraging, the principles expressed so poignantly in letters from a caring father in Hong Kong, survive as a part of Louie's empire today.

They are real, and they have been proudly displayed for the new generation and all the world to see.

CHAPTER 26

Top Line!

WHEN YOU THINK ABOUT IT, there's something terribly negative about 'the bottom line.'

The bottom line of business. Sure it can be a nice surprise at the end of the day, but it can also be a line of monumental bad news.

And bottom? What a horrible word and what a horrible place to be. The bottom line is what's left over.

Money comes in and money goes out and what's left is the bottom line, the crumbs on your business table.

Have you ever thought about turning the whole thing around and working for a *top line?*

At the beginning of the month or the year, say to yourself that what is left over is not going to be good enough for me. I will set a realistic goal and work to meet it.

You're no longer waiting for the surprise at the bottom, you're shooting for the top!

Maybe you won't quite meet it. So make some changes. Maybe you'll beat it. Set higher goals!

I wiped the bottom line from my personal program many years ago. I said no more! *Someone* may be looking for it, but not me.

I'm up at the other end. Soaring with the eagles!

CHAPTER 27

It's a Long Way to London

I LIKE WINNIPEG, MANITOBA. I love the big, blue Prairie sky, Winnipeg's friendly, welcoming people, the positive way the city gets things done.

And what's positive in Winnipeg? Everything from a self-deprecating joke about the city's famous mosquitoes that rise in black clouds each summer from the flatland waterways, to hearing from a fur-covered, frost-encrusted Winnipeg veteran that he's proud to be living in the world's biggest, coldest city. That's not just talking positive, it's a manifestation of raw courage.

On a sparkling spring day, when the last of the winter had gone and the sun flashed up at the aircraft from the pools of melted snow below us, I came into Winnipeg to make a speech.

It was a ridiculous schedule: I would grab a cab at the airport, head downtown, make the speech, mingle with the delegates at a conference, sleep, head back to the airport and hop a plane through Toronto to London — where I would do the same thing all over again.

Before leaving Winnipeg Airport to head downtown, I went up to the Air Canada counter, gave them my name and schedule and said to the attendant: "I'm staying at the Westin. It's very important that I be in London tomorrow night. If there are any flight changes, could you please let me know?" He assured me he would.

With confidence, and nice feelings about the assignment ahead, I took the cab downtown, made the speech, went to bed, got up, caught the cab to the airport to make the flight to London. Another lovely morning.

I walked to the counter, slapped down my ticket and passport and said good morning.

And the attendant told me the flight had been cancelled.

You know the feeling. The blood moves from the top of your forehead, you drop your shoulders, you assume a fighting, protective stance, a kill anyone stance. It's a reaction that's latent in all of us and it comes with the human territory.

But we CAN control it.

Miraculously, the reasoning side of my brain clicked in: Peter, it said, whatever has happened is probably not the fault of this Air Canada attendant, and it will not do you any good at all to blow up, ruin his day, and still not get to London, England.

So I said: "I wish you had called me at the hotel. I DID leave a number."

And he said: "I know, sir, and I'm terribly sorry. But the cancellation came just a short time ago and we didn't have the manpower to inform all of our passengers."

"Well, no problem," I answered. "You can put me on another flight to Toronto and I can still connect."

"There ARE no other flights to Toronto, sir."

I took a deep breath to stabilize my heartbeat, and the reasoning side of my brain clicked in again: Whatever is now happening is not the fault of this Air Canada attendant, Peter, and it will not do you any good at all to blow up, ruin his day, and still not get to London, England.

So I said: "Is there ANY way at all you can help me get to London?" There was a note in my voice that I rarely hear. It comes from way down deep in the pleading part of our anatomy and that too is part of the evolution of humankind.

And he said: "Just a moment, sir." And he left.

I stood there half fuming and half in panic and 20 minutes later — TWENTY MINUTES LATER! — he came back.

"Mr. Legge," he said, "here's what I've done."

I KNEW right then that he had solved the problem and I leaned on the counter and looked deep into his eyes as I listened to the solution.

"In 20 minutes you will be leaving on a plane for Calgary."

"Yes," I said.

"An hour after you get to Calgary, you will be connecting with an Air Canada flight out of Vancouver, which, despite some head winds over Greenland this afternoon, will get you into London just two hours later than the original flight you were hoping to take through Toronto. O.K?"

I leaned across the counter, grabbed his hand, shook it, read the label on his lapel and said: "Thank you, John. Thank you!"

He smiled, and quietly and efficiently checked my bags, made the computer entry and handed me my baggage tags and tickets. I turned to leave, feeling incredibly elated and surprisingly normal.

"Mr, Legge," he called. And I turned. "There are passengers who buy first class tickets and there are others who are first class passengers no matter how they fly. Thank you for your understanding." I felt terrific!

Of course the story proves a point. Is it that you can catch more flies with honey than you can with vinegar? That a soft answer turns away wrath?

Both of those. But in terms we can understand, it proves that it never makes sense to blow up to make your point, to get angry to get what you want.

It wouldn't have worked in Winnipeg and it doesn't work anywhere. You hurt defenceless people by shouting at them. You win by understanding their point of view, by giving them the respect they deserve in the job they have been assigned to do.

Almost always, people will come up with extra effort when there's understanding. Shouting at agents and clerks and receptionists, and those who have the potential to help, will get you quickly to the back of the real or imagined line, a million miles from whatever your destination may be.

Count to 10, then begin again as a rational human being. It made Winnipeg a better place that day and it can make YOUR day, wherever it may be.

CHAPTER 28

Take a Christmas Break

EACH YEAR I LOOK FOR THE CLUES that will help me to discover what actually drives the Spirit of Christmas.

Money is certainly part of it. A big part of it. Bigger, it often seems, than Christ Himself. The symbolism generated by a long-ago Bethlehem miracle is mostly little more than a prop for the corners of ads, theatrical charm for department store windows, the occasional background sound for a wall of electronic seasonal selling.

Survey results vary, but Ronald McDonald, Santa Claus and Bart Simpson probably run in a burger, beard and brain-altered tie as creatures who are immediately recognizable by today's kids. Today's six year olds would say: "Who's the fourth guy?" and put Christ under "Other."

The Christian Festival often appears *not* to be the fuel for all the fun and good feeling. It gets gratuitous thought and may even culminate in a once-a-year visit to an unfamiliar church, but you'd be stretching it to say that we're driven in any basic way by the Christian Christmas. But maybe not?

The modern day journey toward Christmas is a road lit by many small lights. Like those on the tree, they come on one by one as the switches are turned on within us. And the collective light of Christmas is as bright as we ever want it to be.

We turn away from the first lights. They are the abhorrent ads that offer the best loved songs of the season when the last rose of summer has barely faded. It's really too early. But Bing and Perry and Andy and Nat King Cole and all the rest of the voices past and present are triggers. Their voices — and only the network programmers and ad agencies know when they begin — also begin to absorb us.

Christmas Savings! Christmas Specials! Pre-Christmas Bargains! Our early November lassitude is shaken into a realization that it's time again to think about The Day, to rush out and buy something. Or at least look for it.

The lights of Christmas come on in red and green mail, beckon us with gift certificates, plead with us to remember others, tug at our pocketbooks and heartstrings, cajole with smells, tastes, and a thousand textures of tinsel. The chestnuts are not far away. Alastair Sim and the Video Hordes are primed again to shout gleefully from their frosty Christmas Carol windows, in pale shades of computerized colour: "Come back . . . in less than five minutes, you clever boy, I'll give you half a crown!" Ah, distant Dickens!

The weather helps to move Christmas along. Retailers pray for early snowfalls. Enough to make neighbourhoods look like jolly Hallmark cards, but not enough to slow the traffic. Salvation Army people do better in the snow. They ring their bells harder and jump around a lot to keep warm. Is it guilt money we pay as we sweep by on our way into the department stores?

The weather keeps us indoors. There's more time to talk about Christmas Past, to contemplate Christmas Upcoming. Again, no accurate record as to when one member of the family says to the other: "So, what about Christmas?"

The Americans have a fairly organized start to the season. When the last of the pumpkin pie has been consumed to end the celebration of Thanksgiving in the last week or so of November, that's the signal for the start of the New York Macy's Parade and the real beginning of Retail Christmas. It's a considerable piece of Christmas fuel.

The giving and receiving of gifts is important. The knowledge that somewhere out there someone, for absolutely no reason other than it's Christmas, will shower us with hardware, and/or software, is quite phenomenal. Is it the thought that counts? Should one feel any better because it's a BMW and not a box of chocolates? You DID say yes, didn't you? Those gifts of gold, frankincense and myrrh set impossible standards and we've been trying ever since to match them.

Most of us would be lying if we said we didn't have high expectations about Christmas gifts. There's no doubt at all that we really revel in the kind of attention that Christmas affords, as we are hurt by the disappointments it sometimes can't afford!

We accumulate a ton of guilt at this time of year. We could rid ourselves of it by some common-sense discussion, but we don't. And the alternative is that the common sense in us (or as some would say, the Scrooge in us,) gives way again to the accumulation of a ton of debt for things that we didn't need, that very often command an attention span that lasts until about breakfast time on Christmas morning.

So where are we at? A mix of Macy's, music, snowfalls — and MasterCard to the max. Is that it?

We agreed that the lights of Christmas are small, and they blink on when we least expect them. Handel's Hallelujah Chorus on a car radio in the late-night darkness is a light of Christmas. The smell of the trees in a frosty suburban lot and the waves of crimson and green poinsettias in the supermarkets. They too are lights. The texture and sweet juices of oranges, satiny candies, rich cream and spices in the eggnog, mysterious parcels pushed under beds and squeezed into the corners of high cupboards. They are all lights! Cards from friends in distant places. "Another year! Miss you! Love Bill, Cath and Jeffrey, 14 months and fat!" Each card is a light of Christmas.

And the food! How long does it take to thaw a turkey? To cook a turkey? The plip-plop of the cooking cranberries. The sprouts, the mounds of mashed potatoes, giblets chopped into rich, brown, bubbling gravy, the puddings and the pies, the cakes and the cookies. The food of Christmas sparks enormous candlepower.

And how about love? If we ask what fuels

116

Christmas, we should likely ask what fuels the love of Christmas? Very often, it seems to be around more at this time of year than at any other. Something in the air says: "Use the force, folks!" And for the duration anyway, we blot out the woes of the world and give love our very best shot.

Along with the bustle of it all, it is a season when we steal precious moments to think. Because of its positioning in the year — the end of it, and a clear indication of the passage of time — Christmas is when we ask deeper questions of ourselves. "What is life really about?" "How am I doing?" "Is this the time to think more about the family, the bigger world and what kind of a person I'm supposed to be within it?" Maybe in those quiet moments, unlike other times of year, we give love more of a chance. And everyone else, give or take, is doing the same thing.

"Same to you, fella!" Hateful admonition just doesn't work at Christmas.

With love, many lights come on. Love brings the circle closer, gives focus to the season. If we put it first, we are able to tolerate just about anything — from strange ties in our stockings to frazzled nerves in the crowded Christmas parlour!

The search ends round about here, and the clues, predictably, are as many and as varied as we want them to be. Each of us has private knowledge of where our own Christmas really begins, the absorbing feeling that puts shine in our eyes and extra warmth in our hearts.

The power of Christmas, the glow that washes over us, that each of us understands so well, comes when all of that shine and all of that warmth bubbles over — and for those magic hours, minutes and seconds, we really are one, bound together in unique and precious peace.

In another time, the Bethlehem miracle was the fuel that gave birth to and has regenerated the feeling of Christmases ever since. Love did come down, and love has stayed. We can thank God for Christmas.

CHAPTER 29

It's Showtime!

THOSE WHO HAVE BEEN THERE say that even worse than a government audit is the arrival at your front door of a reporter and camera crew from *60 Minutes*.

It's Showtime — and you've never been less prepared for what's to come!

Facing up to the press can be harrowing, but if you remember a few simple rules, you can not only survive, but benefit from the experience. Think of all those viewers and readers!

All of us remember the press briefings of the War in the Gulf. There, in some of the most difficult public relations situations, the Pentagon people and their representatives in the field, were able to tell a lucid story and survive the toughest questioning by the world's media. Each person was prepared, calm, straightforward, honest.

I think they were playing by these rules, which I

have adopted in my business and which you may like to use in yours.

Keep Calm

It may be a stressful experience, but keep calm. Allow yourself time to think about what you're saying. Strive to maintain emotional control of your voice, your facial expressions and gestures. Cameras are fiendishly clever at picking up details like twitching lips and nervous hands. Don't get angry or allow yourself to be drawn into an emotional debate with a reporter. It may generate headlines, but probably not the kind you want.

Keep it Simple

When you are interviewed, use everyday English. Sometimes it may be necessary to read a prepared statement, but, if you have the choice, avoid it. It is far more effective to speak directly to reporters in a conversational tone in your own words.

Expect the Worst

Talking to the media *can* be unpleasant. Anticipate antagonistic questions and make sure you have rehearsed an adequate response. It can be helpful to rehearse with a member of your staff or a friend.

Record the Interview

Some reporters working under tight deadlines will disregard the context of what was said during an interview in order to get their stories to air on time. Most will be less likely to do so if you ask politely to make your own tape recording of the interview.

Negotiate the Ground Rules

Before you agree to talk to a reporter, attempt to find out who else is likely to be interviewed and the amount of time or space that will be devoted to your views in the finished story. Make sure you understand the focus of the interview.

Keep it Short

The average length of a quote in a TV news report is usually no more than 20 seconds. Keep this in mind as you formulate your answers. Talking too much during an interview can increase the chances of your being quoted out of context.

Stick to Your Message

Resolve beforehand what you want to say and, if possible, try to develop a series of key points to express your message clearly and succinctly. Make your points immediately and elaborate if time permits. Never wing it.

Avoid Being Led

Be careful of hypothetical, leading or loaded questions. Smart reporters in search of a juicy quote may try to trip you up by putting words in your mouth or attempting to get you to repeat the loaded phrasing in their questions. One way of responding to trick questions is to make note of them in your response: "I would prefer not to answer hypothetical questions." Then, restate your key message.

Answer directly

Clever or misleading answers during an interview can often backfire. Avoid joking with reporters or indulging in sarcasm.

Watch the Cutaways

During a television interview, keep your expressions neutral while the camera operator does cutaways or wide shots of the reporter and yourself in conversation. Again, the camera can be ruthlessly honest.

Avoid Off the Record

In theory, off the record statements are made to reporters for the purposes of giving background information not intended for publication or broadcast. If you don't want to see something in print, don't say it.

Never say "No Comment"

The reporter and those who see you or read your name will think you are trying to hide something.

Never Lie

Be honest and factual.

Be Responsive

Answer forthrightly, but maintain control at all times — of yourself and of the direction of the interview. This is an opportunity to get your message across. Don't let the opportunity slip away.

Good luck. I'll be looking for your confident, smiling face on *60 Minutes!*

CHAPTER 30

Back to Tavistock Hall

AS I APPROACHED MY 49TH BIRTHDAY, I strug-
gled with the fact that I couldn't 'do it all over again.'
The half century somehow seemed like a bigger milestone than all of the others I had met and passed before.

At 21, you're *there!* Everything becomes legal and
life can really begin. At 30, you begin to get wisdom. Or
so it seems. At 40, you get strange cards and everyone
laughs at your greying hair. At 50? You claim you've
never felt better in your life. But it's an exponentially
larger milestone than any of the others.

I became very stressed out at 49, reflective about
my youth, about the things I might have done. I thought
more about specifics from my past, about people, about
school — the boarding school my parents sent me to
when I was four years old in Heathfield in Sussex.

My parents always thought that Tavistock Hall was
the making of me, and sacrificed much so that I might

attend it and get the best education possible in postwar Britain.

I spent eight years at Tavistock Hall under the watchful eyes and the caring ways of the headmaster and headmistress, Mr. and Mrs. Ray and Maureen Ward.

Unless there's some kind of organized program in place, 10-year reunions and the like, you tend to say goodbye to the old schools on the day you leave them, and that's what happened when I left Tavistock Hall. Over the years, I never went back. I'd been back to England many times after emigrating to Canada, but it was 38 years before I saw it again.

In the summer of 1990, a business group of golfing buddies had planned a seven-day holiday in Little Uckfield, somewhere south of London in a stately, old 1850 British mansion. It had been the home of Lord Neville, former press secretary to the Queen. It was now owned by a Canadian who had turned it into a magnificent 17-suite hotel, surrounded by two of the most magnificent golf courses anywhere in Britain.

The 36-hole twinned courses were carved out of several old farms, but retained much of their spectacular British landscape. Rows of 200-year-old oaks lined many of the fairways. The tee boxes faced a sloping hill where cows and sheep grazed and a turn of the century — pick any one — church peeked through the treetops. We were in awe of absolutely everything.

I hadn't given much thought to our exact location 'south of London,' but I soon realized that here in Little Uckfield we were but 15 minutes by car from Heathfield and my beloved old school, Tavistock Hall.

On our free day, my wife Kay and I rented a car

and decided we'd go and find it.

It was an easy drive to Heathfield through the Sussex countryside and as we entered the little village, memories of those years in that school came flooding back. The old train station. Still there, but now a boutique. The British Rail lines. Lifted, and the space turned into a parking lot. The sweet shop, which as students we were permitted to visit once a week, was still there. So were many of the other shops and offices I remembered. Like many British villages, the world had almost passed Heathfield by.

The school itself was about two minutes out of town and obscured by tall trees and hedges at the top of a long uphill driveway. My heart was pounding as we ascended the grade. I was totally unsure of what we might find.

But I was to be disappointed. There was *no* Tavistock Hall. After 38 years, not a vestige remained. Nothing except the beautiful trees and back for another summer, the rhododendrons. Time had taken its toll and Tavistock Hall, the grounds, everything, was now a mature housing development of Georgian homes and manicured English gardens.

Is was as if something, even someONE very special had died and disappeared. I knocked on a few doors. No one seemed to know when the old school had been torn down, where the Wards were, whether or not they were even alive.

But when you're looking for your past, you try harder.

I remembered the old rivalry between our school and the Skippers Hill Boys' School in the next county.

There was a chance they'd have answers at Skippers Hill.

With most of the day still ahead of us, Kay and I drove the 45 minutes to the old expected battlefield. Was it there? You BET it was! Not only still standing, but looking exactly as I remembered it. Still a boarding school, swarming with little British kids aged four to 14. Had I ever been one of *those?*

I introduced myself to the Skippers Hill headmistress as a former student from Tavistock Hall and asked if we might look around. Certainly, she said.

Musty rooms, views through windows and tons of memories. The playing fields. I hit a 'six' there in a cricket match and scored goals as part of the Tavistock Football XI. It was wonderful to soak it all up on that fine English morning.

As we poked around the old schoolhouse, the dining room, the library and the dorms, the old rivalries that had once existed seemed to disappear.

"Do you have any idea if the Wards are still alive?" I asked the headmistress. "And if they are, where they might be living?"

"You don't know?" she asked.

"No, not at all," I said. "I haven't seen or heard of them for almost 40 years."

She took me by the hand to her office window, pulled the curtain back and pointed to a little bungalow across the street.

"There," she said. "The Wards live right there."

My heart leaped. Kay and I thanked the headmistress for all of her courtesies, and rushed across the street. Astonishingly, Ray and Maureen Ward were not only alive and well, but at home and delighted to welcome us with cups of tea and the kind of outpouring of conversation that bridged all of those years and left us both with shining eyes.

I discovered that morning that Heathfield and Tavistock Hall had gone into new and changing chapters. The Wards were no longer part of that past and neither was I. We had gone on to other things. There's nothing wrong with that, for schoolgrounds or people. And while it can be hard to watch and be part of change, there's really nothing we can do to stop it. The acceptance of life's passages and the challenges they offer is really a big part of what living life is all about.

But there's also nothing wrong with checking out the past from time to time — if only to confirm that it was better then than it is now. If Tavistock Hall isn't there, we can search out Skippers Hill. And when we find it, it can buoy us up for the new directions we must take. And often, it seems, there's an amazing dividend, the Wards with cups of piping hot tea, and shared secrets of those glorious times gone by.

Dr. Tony Campola from an eastern U.S. university said: "Our past is not as important as how we see our future."

I really believe that. And I also believe that life after 50 won't be bad at all.

CHAPTER 31

"Good Morning, God!"

THIS IS A BIT OF A 'HOW TO' CHAPTER. This book doesn't have too many 'how to' chapters. The problem with 'how to' books is that having read them, you tend to forget the rules and one more time you feel let down.

Most of my messages hopefully come through for YOU in the stories that made them important to ME.

Having said that, on with the 'how to' chapter. And no better place to start than morning, the beginning of another great day.

Psychologists say that the first encounter of the day affects the next 20. That's why wives, husbands, kids, cats, dogs and parking attendants often have very thick skins, or moments of controlled deafness!

But it's time for a change.

Start Your Day on a Positive Note

- Say "Good morning, God" instead of "Good God, it's morning!"
- Give thanks for being alive, for the opportunity this new day gives you
- Give thanks for 10 elements — and maybe more — that are part of your life:
  1. Your wife or husband
  2. Your children
  3. Your family
  4. Your health
  5. Your job and company
  6. Your car, or some other prized possession
  7. Your bank account — whatever its current state
  8. The promise of the day ahead
  9. The beauty of nature. No matter WHAT it's doing outside, there is beauty out there
  10. The community, province, state, country you live in
- Do all things today without complaining

Keep Healthy

- Get serious about good nutrition and a balanced diet. I read somewhere that for every pound you add, you also add something like 350 feet of blood vessels to serve the extra weight. That's a lot more unnecessary work for your heart!
- Get 6-8 hours of sleep in a comfortable bed and awake refreshed

- Do 20 minutes of aerobic style exercise at least 3-4 times a week. If you need more information on this kind of activity, read a good book on the subject
- Drink and eat in moderation
- No alcohol at lunch

Continue Your Education by Feeding Your Mind

- Along with the music, listen to motivational tapes in your car. If you drive 10,000 miles a year, that's two months sitting behind the wheel. Phew!
- Read inspirational books every day. See Chapter 2 for more details
- Think with PMA — Positive Mental Attitude — instead of NMA — Negative Mental Attitude
- Establish an affirming, encouraging tone in your voice. When you speak, support your voice. As actors do, send your message to the back of the hall
- Decide today to be positive

Develop Your Own Motto For Success

- All things are possible
- Do it now
- Eliminate the words "I can't" and replace them with "I can!"
- Today, I can "Soar with the Eagles"
- I am a valuable, worthwhile person
- I am creative, capable and quick thinking

Solidify Your Goals, Dreams and Visions: Put Them in Writing

A goal not written down is just a dream. Write down:

- 10 important things you will do today — and do them
- Review your short range (30 day) goals
- Visualize yourself with your goals already accomplished
- Decide to make this day the best, and act accordingly
- Look within yourself! You are unique and special and have within you the ability to achieve virtually anything you can visualize

Don't Give Up
- Be enthusiastic
- Encourage others
- Stay persistent
- Be determined
- You don't have to BE the best, but DO your best
- Count your blessings again
- Never, never give up on your morally, ethically or legally dreamed goals

Up and at 'em, tiger — your day awaits!

CHAPTER 32

Kick the Tires of Your Day

TO CELEBRATE MY FATHER'S 75TH BIRTHDAY, my wife and I thought it would be a great idea to throw a big bash at the Vancouver Golf and Country Club — a night for him, the family, and 250 or so of his close friends and business colleagues.

The program would be simple and memorable. There would be a celebration dinner, six speakers would share for five minutes each their thoughts on a different aspect of father's colourful and varied past, and to top it all, we would have a 12-minute audio visual show full of images from a life well lived.

There were lots of pictures in the old albums, any amount of related material from organizations and corporations that father had been involved with over the years. What we were missing were pictures from his home town in England, a little place called Greenford in Middlesex. It was a place of fond memories for all of us and shouldn't be left out of the show.

As luck had it, I was to be in London with a group of Canadians on a business trade mission four months before the big night, and given this opportunity, I planned to take the time to travel to Greenford to complete the show with pictures from High Street, our old house, the Red Lion Pub, the church in which my parents were married.

Frank Watts, a skilled photographer and dear friend who was part of the British High Commission team stationed in Vancouver and responsible for the huge success of the British Pavilion at EXPO 86, was part of our contingent in London.

We were staying at a small hotel on Jeryman Street in Central London and on announcing to our group the photo assignment that lay ahead, Frank agreed to be part of the project.

Tight for time and not wanting to upset the rest of the mission's schedule, we asked the hotel concierge what time it would be daylight in London. It was October, and having just arrived we were unsure how much daylight was normal at that time of year.

In a proper British response, he said: "It will be daylight at 6:30, Sah!"

Frank and I thanked him and made plans to be on the very first "tube" train to Greenford in order to arrive and begin our photo shoot at the crack of dawn.

It was pitch black when we left the hotel at 5:30. Our only companions on the street seemed to be cabbies, bobbies and lorries on the way to market. After a 15 minute walk and a 40-minute ride on the London Underground, it was still pitch black when we got to

Greenford.

I remembered the old Greenford Cafe near the bus depot and told Frank that if it was still there, it would probably be open. Let's go for tea and toast, I said, and we'll wait for daylight.

The cafe was open and except for the waitress we were alone. She looked up from the counter and in her wonderful Cockney way said: "Oye, you gents are early then. Nobody's ever 'ere before the bus inspector. What'll it be?"

"Two teas and rounds of toast, please," I said.

"Right, guv!"

It was 7:05 and still dark outside when the piping hot tea and toast was promptly delivered to our table. Just at that moment in walked what surely must have been London's most elegantly dressed bus inspector and his deputy.

"You're late," said Frank as the inspector walked by our table. He barely glanced our way, moved on, sat down and ordered his usual.

Ten minutes later and still dark outside, I asked Frank, a fellow Brit, if England was on daylight saving time, as was Canada. Or perhaps London was appreciably north of Vancouver which would have an effect on the length of its days? Neither of us was great on geography.

"Let's ask the Inspector!" I said, and Frank agreed.

"Excuse me, inspector, but could you tell me what parallel we're on here?"

He looked up. "Sorry, sir, but I don't know nothin' about parallels."

"We're from Vancouver, Canada and we live close

to the 49th parallel. We just wondered what parallel we're on *here?*"

The inspector replied without hesitation: "Oh, we haven't had any parallels here since the Second World War. You'll have to check with the Department of Transport for the answer to *that* one." He might have been having us on, but we were certainly none the wiser and it was *still* dark outside.

It was not until 8 a.m. that the thin October light began washing the High Street of Greenford. At which time, with great care, we recorded on film the remembered features of my father's neighborhood. It was a lot of fun and Frank was most helpful.

I've often thought about that event and the people who were involved in it, about the two of us left too long in the dark. The concierge at the hotel certainly *sounded* confident about the timing of London's crack of dawn. The inspector? He was on a *completely* different track. And friend Frank? He did nothing more than come along for the ride.

In this situation, everything worked out, but in another, things may have been quite different. We were really not well prepared when we set off in the tube that morning.

When you have something very special to do, you must ensure that your research is as complete as possible, that you go in well prepared, knowing as much as you possibly can about what's ahead. We'd planned our day on information from the hotel concierge. But a simple, reliable source on the timing of the coming of day might better have come from a daily paper.

It's a drag going through life with the belief that

what can go wrong *will* go wrong. But it doesn't hurt a bit to have a check list, to 'kick the tires' of your day, your assignment: to make sure that your bases are covered. I'm running out of metaphors, but you understand what I mean.

Make your business decisions and your life decisions on complete and reliable information. Write things down and keep the key points in an accessible place. Flight times, addresses, phone numbers, directions, account numbers, names, the date of your wedding anniversary and what time the sun comes up in London in October. You'll be amazed at the added confidence all of these things give you.

We had a great party for my father. Good friends, wonderful food, brilliant speeches — and a slide show that was the hit of the evening. But I should have included the inspector. He would have added a nice parallel touch.

CHAPTER 33

Trust: A Paris Touch

VARIETY INTERNATIONAL is one of the most successful and respected charities in the world. Every year, usually in May, about 800 Variety members from around the world meet for five days to celebrate the successes of the previous year and to dream about the future — how to continue creating innovative ways to raise money for Variety's special children.

As Variety is a global organization, the opportunity to travel around the world to these springtime conferences is an exciting byproduct of being involved.

A few years ago, the 63rd global convention in London, England added, as part of the agenda, a side trip to Paris.

Paris in the spring! We would certainly include it in our plans. With great anticipation, Jeffrey Barnett of Vancouver — who with his twin brother Peter is a principal of the Elephant and Castle Group of Companies in

Canada and like Peter, is a non-stop Variety worker and supporter — set up dinner reservations at Lasserre Restaurant, one of the finest and most expensive restaurants in Paris.

There would be five of us. Jeffrey and his wife Hildi, George Pitman, another Elephant and Castle principal and Variety stalwart, me and my wife Kay.

It was a fabulous evening. The restaurant had been, or still was, an old house. We arrived at the dining area on the third floor by elevator and the roof folded back to leave nothing between us and the exciting air of Paris, the stars in the sky above.

With the food that followed, a seemingly endless array of courses, classic sauces, delicate accompaniments, wines to match every mouthful, it was quite unforgettable.

The time came for dessert, and the presentation of a menu with the restaurant's classic offerings.

And there on the bottom of the menu in very tiny print, the words in chilling English: "We do not accept any credit cards whatsoever." Never had a thought been more clearly expressed!

We couldn't believe our eyes. A meal of gargantuan proportion almost ended and none of us with anything more than the fewest of francs and lots of good old North American plastic.

Our total cash in a quick reconnoitre — as one does in Paris — was 556 francs, which may have been enough for a tip, but certainly wouldn't cover the meal.

In panic, we asked to see the manager to explain our predicament, quite prepared to remain as Paris *plongeurs* for the rest of our lives.

140

He listened to our story and then, quite unruffled, asked for a business card, which I immediately presented.

"No problem, monsieur," he said. "At the conclusion of your meal, we will simply invoice you and expect payment in 30 days."

We whooped for joy and dived into the dessert.

Wow! What trust!

Here was a man who had never seen us before and would not likely see us again, who was quite prepared to assume the risk of payment from a distant country for one of the largest restaurant bills I have ever seen. It was a supremely civilized thing to do and left all of us in awe of the always unpredictable human race and in praise of the proprietor of the restaurant.

Would the same thing happen in Canada? Maybe, we said, but surely not many would risk such a gesture. But then again?

We subsequently learned that in ten years the Lasserre had only been *stung* on one occasion. They offered credit in every sense of the word, but more than anything they offered the trust they believed would be honoured by guests of the Lasserre. We had a superb lesson in the art of fine dining, and the meaning of trust.

We live in a world where unfortunately it doesn't seem to make sense most of the time to put trust to the test. We lock things up, tie them down, ask for payment in advance — because somehow things have got out of hand. It's a great pity.

But every now and then you find someone somewhere who says: "If you want to rob me, go ahead. Whatever it is you take I will replace. What YOU take will remain as an imprint somewhere deep inside you. I hope you can live with that."

Paris in the spring. What a great place for a spectacular dinner!

Lasserre Restaurant
17 Ave Franklin-Roosevelt
75008 Paris

CHAPTER 34

Murray Plays His Strongest Suit

VANCOUVER, like the place where YOU live, is blessed with many colorful characters. Characters rich and poor help to make the fabric of a city, add to its unique personality, enrich our lives.

Some local characters become bigger than their cities. Through the media, their stories spill over into other cities. It is the nature of our society that we get to 'know' car dealers who live hundreds of miles away perhaps better than we know our next door neighbors. Others who promote themselves well become lovable, larger than life characters that stay with us, often for many years.

Let me tell you about how I got involved with one of Vancouver's characters.

I have always believed that it is almost impossible for anyone to succeed in his or her chosen profession without the help of many others — and when I returned to Canada in 1969 after an 18-month tour in the entertainment business, I discovered that I was welcome back — but I also knew I needed help to get started.

The good news was that my Vancouver agent, showman Ben Kopelow had booked me into Ken Staufer's Cave Supper Club on Hornby Street as the opening act to the world-famous Mills Brothers. The Cave back in those days was a very big deal in Vancouver and internationally — so were the Mills Brothers.

The bad news was that I was not really prepared sartorially to be an opening act for the Mills Brothers at The Cave. While artistically I had been successful in England with television shows, radio, dozens of night clubs, U.S. military bases and even the famous Playboy Club in Pall Mall, I came to Vancouver virtually flat broke.

And Ben had booked me to open at The Cave in seven days. I would be on for two weeks, two shows a night and I had nothing to wear.

Enter character Murray Goldman, one of Canada's premiere clothiers, a man who through unique advertising had earned himself that larger than life status. (Outside of business, he used his promotional skills to help Big Brothers, a cause that for Murray never ceased.)

Murray came to the rescue. He invited me to his Hastings Street headquarters and told me to pick out five or six outfits — suits, ties, shirts, whatever I needed. He would have them tailored and ready by opening night.

"Pay me when you can, Peter," he said. "You HAVE to look good at The Cave. And I'll be there opening night to make sure you do."

Well, I opened, and thanks to Murray, I looked

great. And more Cave assignments followed right along. I wish it was still around.

I think what's important in all of this is Murray. One of those people who is ready when we need them to help us along. He trusted me and I walked tall on that stage because of him. Murray didn't ask questions or look for I.O.U.'s, he came right out with a tape measure and went to work.

And, of course, he was there on opening night, smiling as big as ever.

Murray did it in HIS special way and from time to time I guess I've seen opportunities and jumped in to help. I will tell you again and again these are the gifts of self that bring immeasurable rewards; it makes us feel so good that these kindnesses can happen. Too often humans hurt. If only we understood the benefits that come when we reach out to help.

This story remained a secret for many years until the Big Brothers of Vancouver held a roast to honour Murray for his unselfish support for all those years — and asked me to be one of the speakers.

I told this story to the more than 1,000 guests who were there. It was one more way of reimbursing Murray Goldman for the generous contribution he made to my show business career.

CHAPTER 35

Plain Gold Band

'TIL DEATH DO US PART.

It's a phrase of enormous finality, but if you are married, you probably included it as one of the promises you made on your wedding day.

To have and to hold, in sickness and in health . . . 'til death do us part. With the best of intentions, in surroundings that always add great weight to the solemnity of the vows, we commit to live life together. Forever.

Sometimes it works.

My first and only wife Kay and I celebrate our 24th wedding anniversary this year.

There have been some exceptional moments in our marriage. Stories of some of our adventures together are told in this book. But there have been many times when the Legge marriage has been considerably less than a bed of roses. Like any marriage, there have been lots of ups and downs, uncertain moments that severely test the sincerity of our promises.

But 'til death do us part meant exactly that for Kay and me. We would work things out and keep on going — because way back then, we saw something in each other that lit a fire that we believed could burn for a lifetime.

I was virtually flat broke when we were married in England. Eight English pounds was all I had to buy Kay's wedding ring. By any standards, not a lot of money, even back then. But it was a ring that was bright, shiny and made of gold.

When the minister said: "You may put the ring on Kay's finger," it didn't slip on all that easily. But it did go on and found its place comfortably on the third finger of her left hand.

It looked quite marvellous, we smiled at each other, and knew that the ring was indeed a shining symbol of a life together that for us was beginning at that moment.

Over the years, I believe that inexpensive wedding ring has become my wife's most cherished possession. It has some visible nicks and scratches, the kind of bumps and wear that time gives to most everything. On the surface, the lustre of the metal is less than it was on the day we were married.

But the inside of the ring has grown more smooth, as has our marriage over those 24 years. In fact, Kay says that the ring fits better today than it did on our wedding day. Like our relationship, it has molded itself into something closer, something finer, more precious.

The De Beers people say that somewhere along the way in a relationship, we should all be buying the big diamonds we couldn't afford when we were courting.

148

But those of us who are really sharing our lives together give in other ways, and we do it every day. Not with diamonds, but with smiles, with kindness, with touching, with caring. And the small, inexpensive band of gold at the centre of all of this, still works extremely well. Over the years its value has appreciated far beyond mere money. Its value is up there almost beyond understanding.

Life IS commitment. It's making promises to ourselves and to others and keeping them. To our wives and husbands, our children, our larger families. It's commitments in business, the way we DO business, those we serve in business.

'Til death do us part is not life's suprise ending, nor is it the locking of a mythical ball and chain. It is a glorious promise made by two people who have been given the opportunity to live and love together into a future that goes on and on and on.

Kay's ring, OUR ring, shines brightly through the nicks and scratches of time. Like the lady who wears it, it is priceless.

I'm not the lover I once was, but I'm more in love than I once was. Power and glory forever.

CHAPTER 36

The Extra Mile

IN THE LAST 15 YEARS, I have had the very real privilege of meeting all kinds of very successful people. Get close to success, it sometimes rubs off!

Some have been the presidents and chief executive officers of large, prosperous companies, others have been stars in show business. There have been totally motivated platform speakers, sports celebrities, those who gather enthusiastic crowds wherever they go.

Invariably, conversation with these people gets round to the question that each of us asks every so often.

"What single thought best describes the key to a successful life for you and for others?"

To my initial amazement, the answer often comes back: "If someone forces you to go with him a mile, go with him two miles." Or words to that effect.

It is not an answer bound up in what we think of as wealth or possessions. It is an answer about giving. It is an answer about the quality of life. Going the extra mile is about the kind of success you can have in a lasting relationship with your spouse, in the lifelong commitment you make to raising your children, to your community, to all of those giving things that make us human beings different and special.

"If someone forces you to go with him a mile, go with him two miles."

The ring of familiarity? Jesus Christ said it in the greatest address of them all, the Sermon on the Mount. You may re-read it if you wish, in the New Testament. Matthew, Chapter 5, Verse 41.

Going the extra mile, giving more than you have been asked. Sometimes, if you do more than you are being paid to do, you will be paid more for what you do. Sometimes, the reward for the extra mile is nothing more than the satisfaction you get from having done it.

But people who walk that extra mile, no matter what their reward, are a success in every sense of the word. Often they leave us in awe of the very real sacrifices they make and keep on making.

Think of the legacy that Mother Theresa has left the world. Think of the often unrecognized armies of selfless people who go the extra mile in our hospitals, our hospices, who comfort, care, keep coming back.

The tough thing always is to recognize exactly what the standards of life really are, or should be. We get confused, get off track, keep pushing toward goals that entice us mightily, then crumble as we touch them.

But the extra mile? Now there's a challenge.

It takes courage to walk it — but you will find new strength in every step you take.

CHAPTER 37

Going to the Mountaintop

YOU MAY DISAGREE WITH SOME OF THE IDEAS suggested in this book, but I think we will all agree with this one.

Most people confront at one time or another what is often called a 'mountaintop' experience. I'm not talking about the Shirley MacLaine versions, but about all of the special and precious moments in life. The birth of our first child, the final payment on the mortgage, the triumphs in our chosen sports, winning a 10K run, starting a business — maybe something as deliciously improbable as winning a lottery!

But what's the Number One 'mountaintop' experience we could possibly experience? Unless I've completely overlooked something, it would have to be a one-on-one, face-to-face conversation with God. Seriously. No matter what your faith might be, no other 'mountaintop' experience could top this. It would be the summit of experiences.

The trouble with us human beings is that we are tough to satisfy. One 'mountaintop' experience begets another. And another and another.

If we are not careful, we start to look on life as being meaningful only when rare and completely exhilarating things happen. If it's not a total high, we're right down in the dumps.

In the Old Testament, we learn that Moses, who lived to the ripe old age of 120 and was chosen by God to lead his people to the freedom of the Promised Land, had several 'foothills' experiences, but had only one truly 'mountaintop' experience, a face-to-face conversation with God.

And from the mountaintop, he brought down God's Commandments. It was an experience of epic proportion.

But for most of his life, Moses was slogging it out in the trenches. And that's 120 *years* of trenches!

As Moses did, what we have to do is cherish the mountaintops, but learn to understand that it's quite normal and quite O.K. to spend lots of time in the trenches. Ordinary highs are very acceptable.

With the right attitude and understanding, there can be great joy and great satisfaction in what those of less wisdom may see as tedious daily battles.

(Kids are tough. Just watch them charge through the complete pile of presents on Christmas morning, searching for that mountaintop marvel that will keep them completely absorbed for as long as perhaps 10 minutes!)

I think what old age does — is there such a time?

— is slow us down, force us to start smelling the roses that are at our feet, listen with a fading ear to the sound of the soft wind.

Even in the valleys there are mountaintops.

Robert Louis Stevenson wrote much about the journey of life, about success and the way we aspire to it.

As well as cleverly observing that "youth is wholly experimental," he said that success is not a destination, it's a journey.

And there is more from this man who gave us Treasure Island and The Land of Counterpane: "I travel not to go anywhere, but to go. I travel for travel's sake. The great affair is to move." Here's a man who knew and appreciated his trenches.

"To travel hopefully is a better thing than to arrive," he said. "There is only one arrival in life and that is at the end of life . . . All the achievements, the moments of success are merely milestones along the way."

Our only face-to-face 'mountaintop' experience with God, other than our personal prayers, may, in fact, be at our life's end when many of us feel we will be required to give some kind of accounting of the life we have led, the good and the bad.

Mountaintops? Milestones? Trenches? Perhaps there is no better time than now to think where YOUR story might begin — or how you might shape it for the rest of your life.

I'm working on mine.

CHAPTER 38

Do You Have All Your Marbles?

FRANK W. WOOLWORTH, whose vision started a different kind of retail empire and made 'five and dime' part of the language — although inflation has sure made it less meaningful! — said: "I never got very far until I stopped imagining I had to do everything myself."

If you have come this far in this book, I hope that one of the things that may have inspired and pleased you — along with the undoubted value! — is that this is a book about real life, the stories are real people stories. My own. Stories about people I have got to know and whose lives have inspired me.

Prior to the reign of terror in Uganda by Idi Amin, a young man and his family enjoyed building a very prosperous business in the food industry. In fact, in that part of the world, they were considered the Ugandan supermarket leaders.

The young man's name was and is Sadru Ahmed.

Sadru is a human dynamo, full of boundless energy, optimism, enthusiasm and dogged determination.

Sadru is about five feet tall, bald and brown. He says he's bald, brown and beautiful.

As determined and as courageous as he now is, he knew that he and his family were no match for the likes of Idi Amin, and he decided to leave Uganda.

Leaving Amin's terror behind, Sadru smuggled his family out of Uganda. Sacrificing his personal fortune and huge family supermarket business, they went first to London and then on to Vancouver. Left behind was everything he had built. It would become the spoils of Amin and his boorish terrorists.

Starting anew in Vancouver, Sadru looked for a company that would provide a 'fit' for his skills, a company where he could grow and again prosper. He reasoned that if he was ever to be recognized, he must dig deep into the company he would serve. Start at any level and work hard.

He chose an import food brokerage company called National Importers Ltd. He was assigned the task of cleanup man in the company's impressive Vancouver warehouse.

Once on the payroll, his old energy came alive and it quickly became evident to the company owners that Sadru had natural enthusiasm for the food business. His contribution would be valuable. He was executive material.

In 10 years, Sadru was Managing Director of National Importers and the business thrived — he was directing more than $25 million in annual sales.

Sadru could reflect on an incredible decade.

Uganda, and all those memories, were part of distant history. Now established in a land that presented him with rich opportunities — like so many of us who are willing to explore its potential and work toward goals — Sadru had begun again, and won.

I have learned much from Sadru, but the favourite among many ideas he has shared with me about personal and corporate growth is this one:

Delegation is absolutely essential!

He may have learned it from F.W. Woolworth or through his own life experience, but he knows of its importance as part of good management.

When Sadru hires a new staff member, along with the office, the desk and the other accoutrements they receive to help them do their job, Sadru gives them a jar full of marbles. That's right. Marbles. Each marble, he explains, represents a particular responsibility and/or job function.

Then he tells the new executive that from time to time, he will give them *more* marbles. Once a week, once a month, once every couple of months — but they will come.

The trick, he says, is that at no time must the marble jar ever overflow. If it ever does, he'll hear about it.

The choice for Sadru's people is quite simple. From the bottom of the jar, the middle or the very top — before the new job goes in, another job must be delegated out. And the order of the jar is maintained.

What a superb piece of office 'furniture.' Every minute of every day it's a reminder about the importance of work about priorities, perhaps even *life* priorities. That's for the executive to decide. And how much more focused than those ridiculous swinging balls that go click, click, click and eventually numb the best of executive brains.

I could take the easy way out and say that the message in this chapter is: "Don't lose your marbles!" A better one might be: "USE your marbles!" Fill a jar of your own and use them to follow in the clever footsteps of Woolworth and Sadru Ahmed. Sitting there on your desk, they will help you sort things out in the often difficult world of choices that we all have to make. When one marble goes in, one must come out.

With his family Sadru now owns and operates his own prospering food brokerage company. He calls is Jentash Marketing — Food For Thought Ltd.

Isn't that a great name? For me, it reflects the infectious brilliance of a guy from Uganda who perhaps, like you, is making a dream come true. I love him.

CHAPTER 39

"As a Man Thinketh"

FEW THINGS IN MY LIFE have had an impact on me as much as the content of three quotes from James Allan, Earl Nightingale and the Roman philosopher Marcus Aurelius Antonius.

Allen said: "As a man thinketh, so he is." Nightingale said: "You become what you think about." And Marcus Aerelius said: "Our life is what our thoughts make it."

All amazingly similar, all profound, all to the point, all dead accurate. All original? No!

You have to go back to King Solomon's writings 3,000 years ago in the Old Testament's Book of Proverbs to find what is probably the first time the thought was ever expressed.

Solomon wrote: "For as he thinks within himself ... so he is."

It seems absolutely clear to me that it is our daily,

weekly, monthly and yearly thinking that makes us whom and what we are.

And if we are not thrilled with who and what we are, it is obviously time to change our thinking.

Roy Disney said: "When values are clear, decision making is easy," and perhaps the fastest and most effective way to change our thinking and clarify our values is to answer these three questions:

1.   How do you spend your **energy**?
2.   How do your spend your **time**?
3.   How do you spend your **money**?

Your answers will tell you pretty much what your values in life are — and your values in life are what you think about most of the time. Right?

What you think about most of the time you are, or you are *becoming*. So, if you are not thrilled with who and what you are, begin to change your life values by focusing your thoughts — and the rest will follow.

I could go on, but time's a wastin' and I know you have much to think about.

CHAPTER 40

Let's Get Physical!

THERE'S A NASTY RUMOR GOING ROUND, which says that for every pound of fat you add to your body, you also add something like 135 feet of blood vessels to keep that fat nourished.

It's probably true. And goodness knows, it's a depressing statistic. It means that over the years, I've produced enough excess blood vessels to provide a reasonably complete irrigation system for most of California.

It means that for no reason except my inability to control excessive intake, my heart — the only one I've got — has had to work harder than it should. It's unnecessary and it's risky.

And while I continue to be tempted by the beckoning finger of food, I'm doing something about cutting down, about bringing a touch more svelte to the often-flabby Legge frame.

I'm working out. I go to this place called Le Physique, which cleverly structures my life to make me come around to a new way of thinking about fitness.

A ruthless taskmaster called Denis Gagnon sets times and dates for my workouts and asks for the usual courtesies of calling ahead if ever I should consider postponing an appointment. There's no goofing off with this guy. You do it, or have a very good reason why not.

So that you too may benefit from Denis' knowledge, I asked him to provide me with his 10 principles of fitness so that I might include them in this book.

He did, and said that not surprisingly they are very compatible with career goals for personal success. I share them with you:

1.   Assess Your Physical Condition

A building without a foundation will collapse. Before you start, you need a starting point. This solid base of information will include a comprehensive fitness test, a stress test, a physical examination and a blood cholesterol analysis. Knowing these details will lower the risk attached to any program of exercise that follows.

2.   Set Realistic Goals

Short-term and long-term goals will enhance your chances for success. Your goals must be realistic and within reach. Ideally, the good lessons you learn in a systematic exercise program will stay with you as life-long habits. You will *want* to keep on going because you will feel better — and it makes sense.

3. Apply the F.I.D. Principle

Your program should be integrated within the proper framework of Frequency, Intensity and Duration. Frequency based on a minimum of three times a week, intensity determined by a knowledgeable trainer and duration of at least 30 minutes per workout will generate an acceptable level of fitness, producing the kind of results you want.

4. Take the Time

A change in perspective and priorities will guarantee that you have the time to exercise. You can and should consider your fitness as another business appointment, an investment in yourself, your long-term good health.

5. Take Action

Physical inactivity is a habit that can be broken. Changing activities by cross training can defeat the boredom syndrome that may develop. Today's best instructors are conscious of this and can help you overcome it.

6. Find the Professionals and the Specialists

Once you decide to make changes, determine just how fit you want to be. Your objectives can help you set some realistic goals and map out your course. If you have specific objectives or problem areas that may include such things as losing weight, controlling back pain or hypertension, consult a fitness specialist.

7. Go Public

You will probably get support if you let your peers and family know and understand what you're doing. It will also decrease any potential feeling of isolation. By announcing your goals to your peers and family, you will also be motivated to meet your goals and win the praise that will follow.

8. Involve Others

By having your own support group of friends, family and trainer, you will decrease any potential self consciousness that may come from entering a fitness program. An additional benefit will be the genuine warmth and encouragement that comes from this collective group.

9. Concentrate on Your Activity

The rewards of mastering an activity are tremendous. Just getting on a program of activity three times a week is rewarding. Performing the activity to the best of your ability is even better. You'll be looking for more!

10. Imagine Yourself Fit

In the last 10 years or so, visualization has been used a lot to increase the performance of elite athletes. The same principles apply in *your* case. Being fit can enhance your lifestyle and help you develop a positive attitude. Only *you* can decide to embark on a fitness program. Having made the decision and started it, you're on your way to newly discovered fitness and the success that invariably accompanies it.

Merci, Denis! I will do my very best to stick with it.

CHAPTER 41

Making the Most of *OG*ortunity

TOWARD THE END OF 1990, I had the distinct feeling that the first quarter of 1991 in Canada could well be bleak. A combination of winter, the introduction January 1 of a new Goods and Services Tax, the extension and deepening of an economic recession — it didn't look good at all.

Now, I'm the kind of guy who tends to see glasses as half full and not half empty, who looks at life as 4,420 weeks in which something should always be happening, I thought the time might be opportune to do something about injecting a little excitement and some revenue into the first quarter of the new year.

What we needed in my opinion was an event to look forward to and a shot of adrenalin to lighten the gloom. We would bring Og Mandino to town and fill Vancouver's 2,780-seat Orpheum Theatre.

Og is an amazing man and has become a good

friend.

If you're not familiar with what Og is all about, here are some words from his biography:

"He was both a successful salesman and sales manager before serving as president and executive director of W. Clement Stone's Success Unlimited magazine for 15 years. Under his management, paid circulation and advertising revenue increased by more than 2,000 per cent.

His 14 books have sold more than 25 million copies and have been translated into 18 languages and into Braille.

His classic, The Greatest Salesman in the World, is the all-time bestseller in the world in the sales field.

He has won a variety of awards, and, in 1984, became only the 14th individual to be inducted into the prestigious International Speakers Hall of Fame. His appearance on the Today Show at the end of 1990 marked his 900th radio and television interview on the subject of success in the last 10 years.

He is listed in Who's Who in America and Who's Who in the World.

He has captivated huge audiences not only in the United States, but also in Canada, Mexico, South Africa, Portugal, Peru, Colombia, Trinidad, Guatemala, Costa Rica, Honduras, Puerto Rico, Bermuda and the Philippine Islands."

Og is a powerful professional speaker, motivator and author, and I believed he could give all of us a lift in the dark days that seemed to be ahead.

We set the date for Tuesday, February 19. I would be keynote speaker — a good chance to speak again to a

168

large hometown audience. Broadcaster Bill Good, a longtime friend and a professional I greatly admire, would be master of ceremonies.

Once we set the date, we began to set goals. And to involve almost everyone in the company. Og's appearance would be promoted with advertising if necessary, but it would come only after a massive one-on-one sales effort by each one of US.

Ogmania came to town! Or if not to town, then certainly to our offices. We set simple formulas that provided expectations of results. (It always helps to know what's expected of you, rather than making a program hopelessly open ended.)

A network of phone calls tapped the market. Individuals were briefed and corporations were challenged. Faxes were sent everywhere with bios and memos and followup material that would help to close ticket sales.

On December 3, our internal newsletter, Insight, was headlined OGMANIA!! ARE YOU SICK OF HIM YET? Check out these OGisms . . .

OG Day Afternoon
The Wizard of OG
My OG has fleas
The goose that laid the golden OG
Totally OGsome
It's an OG's life
Let's not OGue, Honey
What are the OGs?
OGstanding! OGceptional!
You have an OGligation to sell 50 tickets

The quick brown fox jumped over the lazy OG's
    back
Come OGle OG
The OGony and the Ecstasy
There but for the grace of OG go I
Be OGgressive
Invest in OGriculture
OGga sight!
The search for Red OGtober
Three OG night
Learn by OGmosis
OGment your income

I'm sure you can think of more. But by January 1, 1991, remembering we had just gone through that often unproductive time that somehow infects every business during the Holiday Season, we had all but sold out.

As our troops — not to be confused with those in the Middle East — continued to battle on with their personal sales efforts, we added some print advertising and a one-station touch of radio.

By the time the curtain went up at The Orpheum on February 19, we had a full house. It was a marvellous evening.

Proof enough for me that with the right kind of product — I know you will excuse this inanimate reference to his spectacular personality — and the right kind of promotion, things can happen even in the bleak mid-winter in the middle of a recession.

It was one of those OG things that worked out very well indeed.

CHAPTER 42

Opportunityisnowhere!

BE HONEST NOW, how did you read that headline? Opportunity is nowhere, or opportunity is now here? None of the above doesn't count.

In this book, you KNOW that the second version is the one I like.

But far more important than deciphering titles is the ability, the reSPONSibility we all have to recognize opportunities in life.

Opportunities abound. Recognizing them is not a matter of any particular genius or even luck. It's a matter of looking intently at yourself and your surroundings and doing something creative with what you see.

Don't let it pass by. Do something about it.

John Steinbeck looked intently at the farmers and laborers in and around his hometown of Salinas, California. He wrote The Grapes of Wrath and it earned him the 1940 Pulitzer Prize.

Henry Ford did much the same thing. He looked for and found an opportunity on his father's farm in Dearborn, Michigan, where he began experimenting with power-driven machinery. He helped to put America on wheels and started a new auto economy for Detroit.

George Washington Carver, the son of a slave, also knew how to look for opportunities right where he was — and found plenty. He won worldwide acclaim as a scientist by finding more than 300 practical uses for the peanut, ideas that ranged from instant 'coffee,' to soap and ink, to good old peanut butter.

He made 118 products from the sweet potato, including flour, shoe blacking and candy. He helped his fellow Alabamans develop new sources of income by growing these crops instead of cotton.

You're probably saying to yourself: "Yeah, Peter, pick out the best and make me feel bad. We're not all Steinbecks, Fords and Carvers!"

How right you are. But how often have you seen a good idea come bursting out of your television set, your newspaper, your magazine and said: "I had an idea like that!" Or: "It's so simple, I could have done that."

We get lazy, don't we? We let things roll on by, choosing too often not to get involved. And the good idea goes by default to someone else.

It is people like you and me who must seize the opportunity and run with it.

Opportunity is always NOW HERE. Don't let your good idea drift to the bottom of life's drawer. Keep it right up there on your TO DO list, and don't let it go until you've DONE it. Then look for more.

Opportunitiesareeverywhere!

CHAPTER 43

Be Thankful for Your Troubles

EVERY MONDAY MORNING IN OUR COMPANY, I distribute to everyone in the organization another page in the collection of wisdom we call Insight.

Some people read it, three-ring punch it, and make it part of a permanent collection of thoughts they can refer to from time to time. Others give it a quick read and recycle the paper. I haven't heard that it's used for anything else. Perish the thought!

You never do know how these ideas work, but after a year of doing it, nobody told me to stop, so Insight keeps on going. It's a joy for me to collect the ideas and to know that the thoughts contained within these pages may be useful for the people in our corporate family.

It's true that some of the thoughts are mine and others are purloined from history, literature, the daily paper — or something that caught my eye on the way to work. Bumper stickers can change lives!

The January, 1991, Insight read: "Be thankful for your troubles." Maybe not the most inspired headline to start your week, but that was just the headline.

Be thankful for your troubles, I said, because they provide about half your income. Think about it. If it were not for the things that go wrong, the difficult people with whom you deal, the problems and unpleasantries of your working day, someone else could handle your job for half of what it costs to have YOU doing it.

It's true, isn't it?

It takes intelligence, resourcefulness, patience, tact and courage to meet the troubles of any job. That is why you hold your present job — and it may be the reason why you aren't holding down an even bigger one.

If all of us would start to look for more troubles and learn to handle them cheerfully and with good judgement, to look at them as opportunities rather than irritations, we could get ahead at a surprising rate.

There are plenty of big jobs waiting for men and women who are not afraid of the trouble that comes with them. Searching for people to run the show? Look for people who can make decisions that push things forward, who can quickly turn problems into opportunities.

Albert Einstein often said "In the middle of every difficulty lies opportunity."

The presidents and C.E.O.s who make things happen DO get to enjoy many of life's luxuries, but they earn them by making the most of the time where they serve their companies intensely — looking with wisdom at yesterday's results and moving on well armed into tomorrow's higher ground.

So troubles are positive, aren't they? Be thankful for your troubles. They are part of what you do — a potential pathway to something better.

CHAPTER 44

Minuet at Cecil Green

CECIL GREEN PARK is the name of a magnificent old home on an equally magnificent property at the corner of Chancellor Boulevard and Marine Drive in the Point Grey area of Vancouver, British Columbia.

It was a site well chosen for a fine home. Point Grey is the promontory that forms the southern entrance to Vancouver's spectacular Harbour. It also contains the extensive lands of the University of British Columbia and more recently, the woods, trails and beaches of what has been designated Pacific Spirit Regional Park.

This beautiful house was magnanimously turned over to the university in 1967 and has subsequently been used for conferences, seminars and other public and private functions. Those directly connected with the university have first dibs for reservations, but with lots of lead time, it is available to the public for weddings, receptions and other similar celebrations.

In the spring of 1991, my wife and I were privileged to attend a wedding at Cecil Green where a handsome groom and a stunningly beautiful bride exchanged vows in the estate's garden. Beyond the property we could look northward across the dark green of cedar, hemlock and fir to the Straits of Georgia and the misty-blue softness of snow-capped mountains.

Following the ceremony, there was a champagne buffet in the Grand Hall, where we dined to the sounds of light classics played by a quartet — two violins, a cello, and a large grand piano.

The setting, the food, the music, the occasion — everything was perfect.

Did something go wrong? Not at all. But I learned some wonderful things that afternoon about the grand piano that Monica Pfau was playing, and something of its history — and somehow the collective story seems to "work" for a book like this one.

Jan Ignacy Paderewski was born in Poland in 1860, and as well as becoming his country's first Prime Minister, he is also remembered as an internationally-famous virtuoso pianist and composer.

Paderewski played in the opening season of Carnegie Hall in 1891 and along with New York and many other cities, Jan Ignacy Paderewski — surely a name tht only a mother and perhaps a friendly critic could love! — also came to Vancouver.

As often happens with the best of pianists, Paderewski brought his grand piano with him. And at Vancouver, the last stop on the tour, after it had done yeoman concert service and been carried for many thousands of gruelling recital miles, the piano was put up for sale.

The buyer was the Marquess of Anglesley, who moved it to the Thompson Valley area of British Columbia, about 200 miles northeast of Vancouver, to a place called Walachin.

(I apologize for the interruption, but Walachin was to have been the centre for a bold new enterprise of irrigation. To the best of my knowledge, it didn't work. The venture is recognized today by a highway marker and some ghostly remains that succinctly tell the story.)

All of this happened round the turn of the century. Paderewski had gone, Vancouver was growing and the piano had gone to a new home, to what would undoubtedly be a fair degree of obscurity — distant indeed from the world's concert stages.

It was many years later that Vancouver's Dr. William Gibson initiated a drive to bring the Paderewski piano back to the city. Cecil Green Park was being refurbished in the mid Sixties, and Gibson apparently coaxed or cajoled the residents of Walachin to entrust the piano to the University of British Columbia.

They did, it was brought to the coast, and remains today as an often used, wonderful piece of musical history in Cecil Green Park.

It was 1941 when Paderewski died. He was 81. He would have agonized in his last years as Germany mercilessly overran his native Poland.

But there had been happier times. Over the years, along with his brilliance as a political leader and a musical genius, there was another side to Paderewski. A lighter side.

On his visit in 1891 to New York, he ended up as guest speaker at a polo club. Slightly confused, he is alleged to have said: "You are souls who play *polo*, and I am a Pole who plays *solo!*" Beverley Sills told the story on the PBS broadcast that celebrated Carnegie Hall's 100th anniversary.

On another occasion, a young mother in some major unnamed city had a dream and a wish that her young son might some day become a concert pianist. But her encouragement for him to practice, practice, practice fell on deaf ears.

"If only he could hear and see Paderewski play," she thought. "Perhaps it would inspire him?"

As fortune would have it — forgive me, but it's a turn of phrase that's *always* used in stories like these — Paderewski came to town and the mother bought two tickets. On the evening of the recital, she dressed her son in his concert best and off they went to see the famous man play.

At the hall, distracted by the crowd, by friends and neighbors, she didn't see her son heading off to the stage, drawn to the shining piano that stood waiting to be played.

He climbed onto the huge bench and began to peck out the chords of Chopsticks, familiar to anyone who has ever been close to a piano.

"Who's the kid?" someone yelled. "Get him off the stage!"

"Who'd bring a kid here anyway?"

In his dressing room, Paderewski heard the commotion and the music. He grabbed his coat, ran onto the stage and as he encouraged the boy to keep going, the Polish maestro engulfed the boy with his arms and improvised a spectacular accompaniment around the

178

rhythm of Chopsticks' simple chords.

The crowd cheered and Paderewski and the boy proudly took their bows.

"Don't quit," whispered Paderewski. "Keep playing. Keep practicing. Be persistent."

I don't know whether or not that young boy ever made it to the concert stage. But I suspect that Paderewski's encouragement kept him going, opened the doors that night to a new world of musical appreciation. If nothing else at all had come from that chance encounter, it still would have been a great, great gift.

I thought about all of these things at the wedding at Cecil Green Park — seeing that young couple take their vows in the midst of all of that beauty, hearing the music and knowing a little more about the piano, its history, about the man who gave us the delicate and beautiful 'Minuet in G' and left a piece of priceless history that would keep on making music for British Columbia and its visitors for many, many years.

I suspect that those of us who have been married for 25 years, or even 25 minutes, sometimes think we're as insignificant as Chopsticks on a concert grand, that the world tours and the curtain calls are being taken more often than not by people other than us.

We could think like that. Or we can think differently and hear Paderewski's encouraging words. Keep going. Keep on going. Don't give up.

We could think about the *first* Prime Minister of Poland and think too of the uphill battle of Lech Walesa, that country's *newest* Prime Minister. A new story of incredible persistence. Another Pole giving the world the same encouraging message.

When you come to Vancouver, and sooner or later everyone does, be sure to stop by Cecil Green Park. The folks there will make you very welcome.

Ask to see the piano. And maybe when no one is looking, you might peck out the chords of Chopsticks.

CHAPTER 45

The Big Picture from Gastown

MY FRIEND TOM LOCKE is President and Chief Executive Officer of a company called Gastown Post & Transfer. It's the big player in Vancouver's $20 million editing and film transfer market that supports the city's sometimes volatile motion picture industry.

Tom goes at business with gusto, constantly lifting his sights beyond Gastown Post to a bigger picture — the future growth and security of the *whole* film-support industry. He figures that somewhere along the way, Gastown will get its share of a bigger pie — an approach that seems to be working.

When I asked if he would like to contribute some of his thoughts about success to this book, Tom sent along a note accompanied by a variety of exhibits that give insight into the way he does things. There were notes from speeches, words from others that have inspired him, clippings from stories that have been written about him and the successful Gastown operation. I sorted through them and picked out what I believed were these important points:

- Tom can't stand mediocrity and says that fighting it is one of the biggest battles in life. He shoots for the stars. "Most of us," he says, "fail to realize we don't have to be much better than others to really excel at what we do. A slight superiority is enough to make a vast difference."

- Tom is a guy who says that the challenge for his kind of business is in managing and monitoring growth. And along the way, "we have to be able to determine what are necessities and what are toys, to be able to differentiate between a trend and a fad."

- Over the years, as Gastown has enjoyed substantial growth in a highly competitive industry, Tom has kept an open ear to gurus like Peter Drucker, Tom Peters, Harvey Mackay, Og Mandino and others — sorting out their philosophies, writing the occasional letter to a mentor, to develop a management style of his own.

- There's a need to maintain the right balance between work, exercise and relaxation, says Tom. (He has been playing organized baseball for more than 30 years.)

- Quoting Drucker, he says that being efficient is doing things right — being *effective* is doing the right things. And that refers to the work-relaxation balance as much as it does to the organization of time, the priorities of business.

- In a presentation he made a couple of years ago, Tom told his audience not to get caught up in time wasting activities that may feed your ego, but don't really do much for you or your employees.

• He likes Harvey Mackay's suggestion that we should do what we love, love what we do and deliver more than we promise.

• Managers should break the rules, get out of their ivory towers and get close to their fellow employees. They should roll up their sleeves and pitch in when they're needed. But he cautions that management wandering around should have a purpose that shows you care, and are conscious about what's going on.

• When you're marketing to the outside world, make sure that whatever you're doing has been presented to your employees, that they are committed to what you're doing and will be able to follow up as you expect.

• Learn how to listen. Be sensitive to the needs and expectations of people. Fifty per cent of management is inter-relating with people.

• Share the big picture. At least twice a year, meet with your staff to review market positioning, trends and finances on both a macro and micro level. Knowing what's going on, knowing the company's goals, assists in developing commitment. At Gastown, these are called 'Report Card' days, where current information is compared with that presented six months previously.

• Recognize teamwork, says Tom, it's the cornerstone of success. You can't and haven't done it all alone — share the spotlight! If things go wrong, this must also be shared, "a little garlic with the roses."

• Be pro-active. Get out of the reactive 'me too' syndrome and start pioneering. But be careful. Success comes from quick implementation that follows careful decision making. Tom says that good decisions come from wisdom, wisdom from experience and experience from bad decisions. "But if one can gain experience from someone else's bad decisions, then wisdom will come with minimal pain and minimal financial risk." He calls that the Leach Concept!

• Think positively. Preach it and practice it. It will make going to work enjoyable for you and your employees. (We've said the same thing elsewhere!)

• Be the best you can be. Get the most from every day. Success has nothing to do with I.Q. It's just doing a little more every day. It's aptitude and attitude.

Tom has a piece of writing on his wall that is titled A Thin Line Makes the Difference. It has no source, but he has made its principles key to the Gastown success story.

Part of it says:

"Leaders are wrongly attributed with having greater capacities than the rest of us. The truth may be that their similarities to us are greater than we think, except for their discipline in consistently achieving that extra 10% of whatever they attempt.

"The lesson? First: define the primary, key, basic qualities that are demanded of you by your profession in order to succeed. Second: by discipline, by training, and by performance, become better at doing each of these than anyone else. And third: actually perform at these higher levels as consistently as you possibly can. These will be enough to make you the best in your field!

"A part of an inch, a fraction of a second, a better push-off, or a single erg of energy — this is the stuff of winners. And if we want to, you and I can do that too!"

Yogi Berra, that hulking bear who was the celebrated catcher of the New York Yankees and manager of the Mets, was never short of a quick, great line, which despite the convoluted way it sometimes came out, always seemed to make sense.

"If you don't know where you're going," said Yogi, "you'll probably end up some place else."

Ain't it the truth.

J. Douglas Edwards was less picturesque but just as effective saying much the same thing. He said: "The one common characteristic that all successful people share is that they have their goals and their life outlined in writing."

Do you have your goals and life outlined in writing? A 'To Do' list for today? For tomorrow? Next week? Next month? Or is everything you do a series of surprises? Or are you headed for someplace else?

Let's put a list together that may be helpful.

1.   Goals Give Direction

We *have* to set goals for ourselves. They give us purpose, set us in a known direction, add meaning to what we're doing. Without them we drift, discovering in the not-too-distant future that we've arrived at a destination that is far removed from where we thought we were going.

2.   30 Days at a Time

Some people will tell you to set lifetime goals, five-year goals and yearly goals. But I think our world is going too fast for most of us to look that far ahead. Long-range goals can actually slow you down, may even limit your potential. Long-range goals can give you general direction, but short-range goals create exciting urgency. You can reach the goals you set for a month.

3. Make It Happen!

Goals need to be realistic so you can accept them subconsciously. Some people will tell you to go for the top. *"When you reach for the stars, at least you won't end up with a handful of mud!"* True enough, but it can be terribly disappointing to reach, and never touch. It's more effective to set 30-day goals and make them ALL! Be specific and write them down. There is enormous satisfaction at the end of the month when you can check things off and begin again. Set goals beyond your grasp, but within your reach. *Reach as high as you can, then reach a little higher.*

4. 30-Day Personal Goal

Set one goal each month just for you. It can be physical, emotional, spiritual, material — an activity or an achievement. It can be something to gain, or something to lose. Lose three pounds. That's 1 1/2 ounces a day or as much as 36 pounds a year! Get out of bed 15 minutes earlier each morning. THAT adds up to more than 90 extra hours of work or fun in a year!

5. 30-Day Family Goal

Make sure your family benefits from your work. Set goals that will bring you and your loved ones closer to each other. Some examples? Plan a special trip together. Set aside a night each week as family night — and if you're brave enough, suggest trying it without television! Go to a park and take a bat and a ball or a frisbee.

Divide up the work and clean the house. Follow up with a restaurant dinner together. The goal is simply to do it.

6. **Goals Should Be:**
   - Specific — clearly defined and measurable
   - Realistic — where you are now, where you want
                 to be
   - Worthy — of real value to YOU
   - Short Range — 30 days is long enough
   - Attainable — within your present situation

Set goals. They will help you to know where you're going — and you will end up in exactly the right place!

CHAPTER 46

Good Heavens, It's Friday!

IN ITS ISSUE OF MAY 13, 1991, *Time Magazine* had an exclusive four-page spread of coloured pictures that for the first time showed the world what they described as the top secret inner sanctum of the Central Intelligence Agency.

This was the home of the CIA! That always-mysterious collection of spies, analysts, scientists and several unidentified others had revealed their place of work for all to see.

They were striking pictures. Lots of technology, paper shredders piling up mountains of no-longer-needed information, people watching any number of simultaneous television newscasts, people relaxing in a session of Tae Kwon Do in the basement — an interesting, busy place that until now has been well hidden from the world.

But perhaps the most interesting picture of all was a

shot of the door of the Historical Intelligence Collection — a room presumably full of data.

The encouraging thing about the picture was that here in this place of ultimate secrets was a door that was loaded with fun. In this place of endless seriousness, the CIA showed the world they too could smile at the office.

"Let the BOSS do the work!" said a sign taped to the door. "This Project is So SECRET Even I Don't Know What I'm Doing," said another. Someone else had added a Mickey Mouse magnet. There was a cartoon from what might have been The New Yorker or possibly Playboy. Another sign said: "Are We Having Fun Yet?"

Spying, even in its most secretive places, has a lighter side and I thought it was terrific!

Which leads me rather nicely into more discussion about the office, the place where many of us spent a lot of time — and where too many of us have too few laughs.

Recently I read how regrettable it is that so many people who work in offices give a whoop and a holler once every week and shout with relief: "Thank God It's Friday!" It has become the cry of hope for millions who have a desperate need every Friday afternoon to be somewhere else.

I too think it's regrettable. Don't get me wrong, I like a couple of days off as much as the next person does, but I also enjoy what I do in the office — and I do my darndest as leader of the group to make sure that the 100 or so people who are part of our company team enjoy what THEY'RE doing at the office.

I think it's quite O.K. for people to say: "Thank God It's Friday!" But not necessarily with a whoop and a holler. Work shouldn't BE that bad!

It's always been quite natural for me to attempt to try to create a relaxed office. And I don't think it has anything to do with the fact that I once made a living as a comedian. I think that if you put a happy office next to an unhappy office, the happy office would end up being a better performer, the people would be shown to be more creative, there would be less sickness — any number of positive things can result from doing things with a smile.

I feel terribly sorry for offices where the C.E.O. comes in every morning with his or her head down, briefcase in hand — heading again for a non-communicative day behind a closed door. People like that really haven't progressed much beyond the management style of Ebenezer Scrooge!

My group can correct me if I'm wrong, but show me a boss who says hello, knows his or her people, does a little management by walking around, takes time to listen to the things people say are important, and I'll show you an office where Friday comes, but you don't necessarily have to thank God that it's happened.

No big thing, but we work at being happier.

You will have read elsewhere that I circulate a one-page piece of current thinking to everyone in the company every Monday morning. Some of it's mine, some of it comes from others. I do it because I care about people.

We have golf tournaments, bowling tournaments and parties with a fair degree of regularity at our office.

When T.V. Week, one of our magazines, has its annual Awards Night — a salute to the stars of the local media — everyone from the office goes along. We pick up the tab for tuxedos for the guys and provide the funds for a hairdo for the girls. I apologize for what I just realized seems like a terrible imbalance!

We've sent people off for a weekend in Las Vegas for no other reason than it's a great place for a refreshing weekend.

For the company's 15th anniversary in the spring of 1991, everyone went to Hy's Mansion, a wonderful Vancouver restaurant, for a reception that included a draw for 15 prizes with a value of $5,000 — the big prize being a 25" television set.

Later that evening, the senior management group — and there will ALWAYS be extras for those who must assume greater corporate responsibility — were guests for dinner at Trader Vic's. I presented each person with an Inuit carving of substantial value that hopefully expressed my thanks for the job that each had done in the previous year.

All year long, we accumulate photography that ends up as an audio visual presentation at the annual Christmas Party. The show has become a tradition, a production that helps to hold our office family together.

Policy manuals? I figured when I went into business that people learn about the business by talking to each other. You need a manual to learn how to boot up the computer, but you don't need a lot of Thou Shalts and Thou Shalt Nots to work together.

In another chapter, I talked about how we collectively sold out the Orpheum Theatre presentation of super salesman Og Mandino. It was a challenge, but it was fun. And I think the people at our office are always ready for the unusual — like Og motivational signs in the washroom, an Og note slipped in with the payroll.

With pride we give everyone a birthday card that is signed by everyone. The cost is negligible, the thought is priceless.

If anyone in the company wants to take a course to upgrade the job he or she is doing, we pick up the tab when the course is completed.

I think I'd drive people crazy if I went round the office cracking jokes all day. For a comedian it's always a temptation. But that's not what a happy office is all about. What I try to do is work some kind of a push-pull thing where people know that they have work to do, but that what they do is truly appreciated.

Like the door at the CIA, a lot of our walls and computers are adorned with touches that reflect personalities, that offer a reminder that there's a baby at home, or a dog that's waiting for a run, a vacation that's remembered. Pity all of us if these touches were to be forbidden in the cause of 'design' or 'clients' or 'protocol.'

I like it when people stimulate meetings with new ideas, when they stop me in the hall and say: "How about this, Pete?"

I like it when people tell me they climbed a mountain on the weekend, or rustled up the down payment for a new home, or baked bread, or watched Judy whack a ball out of the park. When this kind of information can be shared, we ARE a family. A family committed to business goals, respecting each other's positions, talents and tasks.

The man who wrote that he regretted the universal enthusiasm for T.G.I.F. concluded HIS chapter on the office by quoting the slogan, "Contented cows give better milk" — a line used for many years by the Pet people.

In my wildest dreams, I could never think of the people at our company as cows. And even if I could, I really don't think that the quote does justice to what we have achieved as a corporate family and how we will keep on doing it in the future.

For my money, it's as simple as being honest with each other, doing things to show that we care, that we understand.

Our work gets done — and we smile.

And Friday? Good Heavens, it's FRIDAY!

CHAPTER 47

"No Man is an Island"

ON MAY 15, 1991, the Sales and Marketing Executives of Vancouver named me the 1991 Marketing Executive of the Year. It was a great, great honour and I will cherish it for a long, long time.

What made me feel so very proud was that in the 30 years the award has been made, the recipients have been a virtual Who's Who of business success in British Columbia. People like Jimmy Pattison, the incredible B.C. businessman who headed up EXPO 86 in Vancouver and who is mentioned elsewhere in this book; Patrick Reid, who was EXPO's ambassador to the world and whose personal enterprise helped make it the international success it was; Ron Marcoux, who heads up McDonald's in Western Canada; Rhys Eton, the CEO of Canadian Airlines.

And now I have joined them — formidable companions in a very select group.

The black tie awards banquet was held at Vancouver's plush Four Seasons Hotel with more than 200 of my peers and colleagues in attendance in the packed Park Ballroom. I was deeply moved by the award, and truly delighted that my old friend Maggie Thatcher had taken the time to send a letter of congratulations.

Above all, I was touched by the continuing support of all of those people who came to make the evening so memorable.

This closing chapter, I thought, might be a good opportunity to present one of the stories I told that night in accepting the marketing award. It may give you an additional insight into why nice things like marketing awards, and success, happen.

Several years ago, a young married couple and their young baby lived on the 12th floor of a modest downtown apartment building. They were full of anticipation of the fruitful and abundant life that lay ahead of them in Canada.

Their new life together was just beginning but showed great promise. The husband had a good job with lots of prospects for advancement. He was determined to be a good husband and father, having taken seriously his vows to love and cherish his wife and now baby girl, to be the provider and head of the family.

One winter evening, the apartment building caught fire. Accepting responsibility, he told his wife to stay in the apartment while he went for help.

The fire trucks came, but their ladders were unable to reach the 12th floor. For the mother, now alone in the apartment with her baby, the wait for her husband seemed like an eternity. When he failed to return, she sensed that something terrible had happened and was continuing to happen — and that the fire was dangerously close.

Not wanting to open the door into the smoke-filled hall, but quickly sensing the need for protection, she took her big, black winter overcoat, soaked it in the bathtub, tucked the baby close to her chest, covered them both with the coat and huddled in a corner to await whatever might happen.

The husband died in the fire.

The mother and baby were saved, but protecting the baby, the mother was severely burned. The flames had seared her face, head and hands.

After months of painful surgery, the mother was reunited with her baby girl, determined to do all she could to provide, as best she could, a clean and comfortable home. And while she would be scarred for life and often shunned by society, she would do whatever she had to do to help her baby girl grow up with the best she could offer.

Only the most menial work was available — taking in laundry from her neighbours, scrubbing stairs, work of low pay and low stature.

But she provided, and her daughter grew up in a home, without frills, that was clean and safe. The child was well fed, her clothes were the best that her mother could buy.

The girl graduated from high school and the mother, continuing to do everything possible to ensure the success of her daughter, paid her way to university.

As a freshman, the girl — possessed of all the right stuff — was rushed by a sorority. The girls in charge asked if they could call at the girl's apartment at 8 p.m. to escort her to the sorority house. She said no, not the apartment. She would meet them in the apartment lobby.

At 7:30, wanting to surprise their new inductee, the excited sorority girls talked their way through security, found the apartment and knocked on the door. Not expecting anyone special, the girl answered and the sorority girls burst into the room.

At the kitchen sink, the girl's mother was hunched over the dishes. She turned at the sound and the sorority girls froze when they saw her scarred face.

"Who is . . .who is SHE?" asked one of the girls.

"Oh, she's nobody," said the daughter. And grabbing her coat, she hustled the visitors from the apartment.

"She's nobody!" Can you imagine how the mother felt? The fire, the agony of healing, the years of suffering and giving and sacrificing. A nobody?

For 19 years, the mother had done all she could to raise her daughter to ensure her success in the world, and at the precise moment when loving recognition was not only deserved but demanded, she had been completely rejected.

I would like to be able to tell you how the story ended, but for that we must use our imaginations, and only hope that somehow that young lady grew to understand how incredibly important her mother had been in the success she doubtless achieved.

All kinds of people, whether we know it or not, make sacrifices for US. They certainly made them for ME.

I was honoured as Sales and Marketing Executive

of the Year for what I presume were real and perceived achievements. But it wasn't just for me. There's no way in the world that I could have done what I did alone.

In my current business, in the things I have done before, in my years of growing up, there have been hundreds and hundreds of men, women and certainly children who have unselfishly sacrificed their time, their energy and their talent to make it possible for me to enjoy a level of success in Canada.

My family — my wife Kay, my daughters Samantha, Rebecca and Amanda — my larger family, my friends, associates and mentors, those who head divisions and departments of the company, every member of our corporate team has contributed to my success and helped to make the award possible.

As I did on the night of the presentation, I again salute and thank them all.

You may have come to this realization long ago, but it is almost impossible for anyone to succeed without the help, encouragement and support of others.

The English poet John Donne wrote with great perception several centuries ago that no man is an island, entire of itself. It is an often quoted line because it is so very true.

"Every man," he said, "is a piece of the continent, a part of the main . . . any man's death diminishes me, because I am involved in mankind."

I sincerely believe that my life works in exactly the same way. It's impossible to go it alone. We are creatures who thrive only when we are part of the main, ready to accept what others always seem ready to give. And I have been given much.

Look carefully at those who are pushing you onward and upward, and be ready always to extend a hand and to offer them thanks and give them the same kind of encouragement.

In life, our opportunity is to accept and to give in return. There is no other way.

To do just that completes the wondrous circle that helps to make humanity what it really can and really should be.